So, You Want to Be a

Brendan O'Mahony

Chartered Psychologist

Registered Forensic Psychologist

Version 1.1

ISBN-13: 978-1482011814

This well needed book examines forensic psychology careers through the eyes of trainees, qualified forensic psychologists, academics and supervisors. Significantly it also gives accounts of the reasons why two trainees commenced the training route but abandoned it prior to completion to follow other careers.

The book is written by a forensic psychologist who has previously worked as a careers adviser and this combination of experience makes this essential reading for any undergraduate considering this career and indeed for anyone interested in forensic psychology training in the UK.

'I cannot express enough about what a great idea your book is and how useful, how helpful it is. I wish I had seen it before I went to my (MSc) interview; I still made it through, but I could have been better prepared. And you even have useful websites at the end. Specifically the ones for jobs are really good... '
A.W., psychology graduate (2012)

'This is an excellent and thought provoking book for all undergraduate and recent graduate psychology students who are seeking additional information about a career in forensic psychology – very well written and extremely useful'

Dr. Gavin E. Oxburgh, HCPC Registered Forensic Psychologist & Senior Lecturer in Forensic Psychology, Teesside University

'If you're considering a career in forensic psychology, this book will be very helpful to you. It provides first hand experiences of trainees, qualified psychologists and supervisors and a good overview of the different routes towards getting qualified. It should help you decide whether forensic psychology is the career for you and help with any applications you are making for assistant or trainee roles.'

Nicola Bowes, Forensic Psychologist and Senior Lecturer at Cardiff Metropolitan University.

Contents

Disclaimer

This book has no affiliation to The British Psychological Society, the Division of Forensic Psychology or any other organisation. The content and comments within are purely those of the author and those named and anonymous contributors who have assisted him in this venture.

Readers must ensure that they seek the most up to date information about accredited training from the British Psychological Society and the Health and Care Professions Council.

Acknowledgements

I would like to offer my sincere thanks to all contributors to this text: to those who completed questionnaires and to those who allowed me to interview them or who provided a written account of their experiences. I am sure that readers of this book will appreciate the time that you have given to make this information available.

Abbreviations

BPS - British Psychological Society

DFP - Division of Forensic Psychology (BPS)

FPiT - Forensic Psychologist(s) in training

GBC - Graduate Basis for Chartered Membership

GBR - Graduate Basis for Registration

HCPC - Health and Care Professions Council

HMPS - HM Prison Service

MDT - Multi-Disciplinary Team(s)

Preface

This book is aimed at filling a gap in the market for undergraduate and recent graduate psychology students who are seeking additional information about a career in forensic psychology. This book is not intended to be an academic read but rather more 'chatty' in style and it does not claim to have answers that may represent the full spectrum of opinions that one may hear from each and every trainee currently enrolled as a forensic psychologist in training. I feel that I am as qualified as anyone to write this text having previously trained and worked as a careers adviser.

My intention in writing this book is to provide an easy read source of information for potential forensic psychologists in training that 'tells it like it is'. Throughout the book I have signposted other places where the reader can gain additional information about postgraduate training. I hope that you will enjoy the book, that you will have a real opportunity to reflect on your individual needs and aspirations and that you will make a considered decision when choosing the next stage of your personal and professional development.

Before you start reading this book I have one small request to make. I would urge you to spend a little time reflecting on your current knowledge about the work of psychologists. How much do you actually know? Who have you spoken to? I have set aside a few questions for you to reflect on prior to reading the main text. Finally, please email me any comments that you have about the usefulness of this publication.

Brendan O'Mahony
January 2013

Email: info@traineeforensicpsychologist.com

15

Knowledge Check: No pen required!

What type of establishments do forensic psychologists work in?

What tasks do they do on a daily basis?

How much of what I know has been influenced by what I have seen on TV and in films?

How does the work of a clinical / counselling / occupational psychologist differ to that of a forensic psychologist?

Is it possible for me to work in a forensic environment without being a forensic psychologist? If so what are the other jobs that I ought to research to make sure that I am making the right career choice?

Part 1

Chapter 1: Introduction

Whilst browsing the internet one Sunday afternoon looking for information about forensic psychology training I quickly realised that there was very little information available outside that which is provided on the British Psychological Society's website. I did find links to various UK university psychology departments but nothing that was independently written by those who had worked so hard to qualify as forensic psychologists, aimed at those who were either on the route to chartership or those who were considering a career in forensic psychology.

Knowing that there was already a published resource book for those considering clinical psychology training (Knight, 2002), the thought crossed my mind that there was room on the market for supplying further information to those seeking a career in forensic psychology. This view was cemented in my mind when I received email correspondence following an article that I had published in *Psychologist Appointments* in April 2007. I had written this article about my experiences in changing careers from the police service to psychology and about my ongoing experiences in trying to get chartered as a psychologist. I received several emails from individuals who thanked me for writing that article and all of them requested further advice and guidance from me.

Another reason that has inspired me to write this book is that many undergraduate students and recent psychology graduates have contacted me over the last few years asking my advice about training and entry to the profession. A recent example of such contact which highlights a need for support follows:

I have been applying to trainee forensic psychology positions advertised both on jobs.ac.uk and through the HM Prison website. Unfortunately, I am always told that whilst I have an impressive CV I do not have enough experience. I understand this, but I have been unable to find a psychologist either willing to allow me to shadow them or a psychological department willing to talk to me. I am trying to volunteer on the Youth Justice Board and also for Victim Support in hopes to gain some experience to permit me entrance onto an MSc, again they are put off by my lack of experience. I was wondering if you may have any ideas as to people who may be willing to give a little time to either pass on useful information as to career development or either in providing work shadowing or voluntary opportunities

Other comments that I have received that continue to inspire me included:

"I think your website is a great idea and just what a lot of people have been waiting for"

"I am a third year undergraduate studying psychology. I would love to go on and train as a forensic psychologist; however, I am completely clueless how it all works really. Once I complete the MSc in Forensic Psychology, how do I go about getting a placement as a trainee? I have searched job websites but there are none advertised on

there – are they that rare? I think that having a website dedicated to forensic psychology is an excellent idea! Maybe it can help people understand the process a little better!"

Whilst I always try to answer such queries as best as I can I also ensure that all interested parties make reference to the British Psychological Society's main website, and more specifically to the Division of Forensic Psychology web pages. It appears to me that an assumption is made by lecturers and applied psychologists that all students know exactly where to seek advice from. This is clearly not the case and it is with this in mind that I have written this book so that you realise that you are not alone in your struggle to make sense of the training route! I wasn't surprised to read that a recent survey conducted by the Division of Forensic Psychology found that 70 per cent of respondents who were General members of the Division were unaware that the DFP website existed! (Forensic Update 108, October 2012).

So, I drafted the skeleton for this book and created a website with questionnaires that could be downloaded for a survey with the aim of assisting those considering a career in forensic psychology to make informed choices. This book is the result of that early work.

I want to encourage any reader who has a dream, to follow it through. I want to encourage you to be assertive in making contact with people as the competition in this field is strong and you need to stand out from the crowd. I will now take you on a brief journey of the history of the Division of Forensic Psychology and illustrate how the profession is growing at a fast pace. Competition for training places is fierce. The Division of Forensic Psychology came into existence in 1999 having taken over from its predecessor named the Division of Criminological and Legal Psychology, which had been in existence since 1977. At that time membership of the division was 105 whereas by 2008 membership stood at 1,996.

In 2007 when I began examining the membership figures there were 762 full members (Chartered) of the Division of Forensic Psychology with 823 members in training and 238 *General* members (Total 1,823 members). These figures are staggering and show that there were more people in training than were actually qualified and indicate the growing popularity of this career choice. More recent figures obtained from the DFP in September 2012 show that there are currently 2,534 members of the DFP who are registered in three categories; 913 Chartered, 487 In-Training, and 1,134 who are described as *General* members. The *General* member's category appears to have increased significantly since 2007 and is likely to include people completing MSc courses but who are not yet registered for Stage 2 of training. When we compare the current figures to those from 2007 we can see that there are more qualified members now (913 as opposed to 762) and less people in training (487 now as opposed to 823). These figures do not however enlighten us as to how many people have commenced training but have subsequently left. This book is intended to supplement the information provided by the British Psychological Society and not to replace it. The philosophy of this book is that it will be a useful resource, a reading experience that challenges your knowledge, and ultimately a book that provides useful information in a supportive and positive manner.

The process of obtaining qualified status as a forensic psychologist has changed over the years. I qualified through the "old route" where I had to spend a minimum of two years, after achieving my MSc in Forensic Psychology, working in a supervised forensic psychology post where it was possible to demonstrate after this period of time that I had acquired both depth and breadth of relevant experience in a forensic setting. You will get a chance to read more about the current route to qualification later in this book when reading accounts provided by other contributors.

Whilst I obtained a post as a trainee forensic psychologist in a medium secure hospital many people choose to work in the prison service. It took me nearly three years to acquire enough experience to be able to evidence the material required to complete an application form for full membership of the Division of Forensic Psychology, which is a division of the British Psychological Society. My application form had to be refereed by two chartered psychologists who agreed that I had met the appropriate standard to practise independently as a psychologist. I had to demonstrate competency in assessment and treatment, research, communicating psychological knowledge and training other professionals in psychological knowledge.

I was very fortunate to be supervised by a very experienced forensic psychologist who had worked in the prison estate, with young offenders in the community and who had the additional experience of being a member of the Parole Board for England and Wales. You have to put your faith in your supervisor throughout the training period and be ready to accept constructive feedback throughout the supervision period as you develop the skills required to assess, treat and write risk assessment reports of a standard high enough to attend court, parole board hearings or Mental Health Review Tribunals.

It was a steep learning curve for me and a very memorable period in my personal and professional development. Before you commit to this kind of training, I think that it is essential that you speak to others who have gone before you. I have tried to simplify this task for you by making contact with some trainees who have been prepared to tell you the good things, as well as the challenges of training to be a forensic psychologist. I hope you enjoy the journey through this book and are furnished with a little bit more information when making an important career choice. One thing that I can't do though is create job opportunities. It does seem like there are fewer opportunities available at the moment in the public sector and unfortunately I rarely see advertisements for forensic psychologist in training posts. It is to be hoped this position will change as the economic climate improves. There are currently too many people chasing too few opportunities and as one graduate about to commence her MSc has commented:

I have been writing to Supervising Psychologists (the ones listed on the BPS site), to many HMPS area psychologists, to the Probation service and to NHS trusts. Some people are nice and actually get back to me. I have even offered to pay people an hourly rate to let me shadow them but they say that due to confidentiality reasons it isn't possible. How can I progress?

I know that it is so difficult to remain optimistic when doors seem to be closed in your face. I can only urge you, if your personal and financial circumstances allow, to be creative and to seek as much relevant experience as you can whilst the psychological assistant and trainee posts are few and far between. Undoubtedly there are confidentiality issues but it is possible to address these in certain circumstances. For example, if an independent psychologist gained permission from the instructing solicitor / prison and the offender being assessed then it should be possible for a psychology graduate to shadow a forensic psychology assessment. I tried to arrange such a visit recently with an MSc student who contacted me. The solicitor agreed to the proposal but the offender in prison said no and I, of course ,respected the offender's wishes. The MSc student was of course disappointed but I think there was even a learning point here that could be discussed about the importance of informed consent and offender choice. Even though the visit didn't materialise for the student there was material that could be discussed at a future interview. Whilst in training I accompanied my supervisor to a Parole Board Oral Hearing and so long as it is arranged well in advance it can be done. So while the opportunities are scarce you might consider occasionally trying to get to see a forensic psychologist in practice whilst you gain some valuable experience that is relevant, but not directly supervised by a forensic psychologist.

Chapter 2: My long winding road to qualification as a psychologist

It is fair to say that I have taken a rather unconventional route, over a number of years, to achieve Chartered status as a forensic psychologist (and since 2009 the status of Forensic Psychologist registered with the Health & Care Professions Council). This may reassure the mature student who seeks a career change. It may also worry the new graduate who might question the need for so much work experience prior to commencing training as a psychologist. I would urge you to fear not.

My interest in forensic psychology was nurtured by a previous role that I had with the police service. I used to train police officers about investigative interviewing, a term used in the policing world to describe how best to interview witnesses to crime, victims of crime and police suspects. Whilst I had a good grasp of knowledge to train skills in this area I found myself referring more and more to the theoretical background of such interviewing practices. I commenced an MSc in Forensic and Legal Psychology and after two years of part-time study I completed my dissertation on the topic of investigative interviewing.

Having left the police service I really struggled to find employment as an assistant psychologist. I encountered some scepticism from potential employers about why I would want to work for a low salary whilst finding my feet in the world of psychology. I spent about one year working a few hours a week as a volunteer with a local youth offending team and I guess this experience was the foot in the door that I needed. Whilst attempting to gain a psychology post I trained as a Connexions Personal Adviser where my role included offering support to adolescents who had behavioural and emotional difficulties. I became frustrated with this role because I had to refer young people to mental health services for psychological intervention as their needs were outside my skills and knowledge base and it made me even more determined to secure training as a psychologist.

Meanwhile I continued to scour the web and the press for job adverts. I applied for a number of assistant and trainee posts and even attended several interviews. With the benefit of hindsight I know that I was naive when completing some application forms and attending interviews. For example, I applied for an assistant psychologist post with the NHS in a role where the client group had learning disabilities. During the interview I was asked the question "What do you understand by the term 'Valuing People'?" I gave a considered reply not realising that there was a published document with that title relating to persons with a learning disability and my poor preparation for interview was immediately recognisable to the interviewing panel. I have provided a couple of references at the end of this book, which I hope will be helpful to you when researching jobs. The feedback that I received following interviews was usually the same. "You have lots of experience, but none of it directly involves applying psychological theory and practice to the offender population." How frustrating! I became used to the standard reply:

Dear Mr O'Mahony

Psychological Assistant Vacancy

Further to your recent interview at this establishment, I regret to inform you that you have not been selected for the position of Psychological Assistant on this occasion.

Thank you for your interest

Here is another example of a letter that I received following an unsuccessful interview for a post as a trainee forensic psychologist:

"During interview it was noted that this candidate was able to present awareness on a number of issues relevant to forensic practice. His answers relating to motivation and commitment lacked depth in reasons as to why he wished to work as a Trainee Forensic Psychologist and demonstrated insufficient competency in this area. During interview he also lacked the ability to demonstrate his ability to utilise feedback for his own ongoing improvement."

And an example of feedback received following an unsuccessful interview for a Psychological Assistant post at a Young Offenders' Institute:

"During interview you were assessed as performing most highly in the areas of communicating clearly and rehabilitation orientation. The board noticed that you performed less strongly on team playing and liaison and adopting a systematic approach."

Other frustrating, but excellent feedback that I received included

"Although you obviously have a range of experience and skills in a number of areas (education, guidance, social work, police, etc) it was not always apparent from your responses that you were clear how you would distil and focus these onto forensic work in psychology. Similarly, your experience was conveyed as teaching and leading colleagues towards general outcomes, rather than presenting as managing staff and processes with specific aims and objectives in view, related to psychological and forensic experience and knowledge.

"It may be useful to review your experience and to identify those areas that you can highlight as related to specific psychological theory, issues and interventions"

I have included these extracts because they may assist you to prepare thoroughly for job applications and interviews. Always ask for feedback from interviews and try to take on board that feedback.

My lucky break came after being turned down again for an assistant psychologist post. I was competing against two candidates with First class honours degrees in psychology, one of whom also had an MSc in forensic psychology. I volunteered to take a part-time unpaid post if necessary with that organisation in order to get my foot in the door. That was the best move I ever made in terms of entering the profession of psychology. Within three months I had applied for and secured a post as a trainee forensic psychologist within the same organisation. I was to spend more than two years in post completing my training in this hospital environment. You may be forgiven for thinking that it is all plain sailing from then onwards. You will still need a determined attitude to achieve all the requirements necessary to meet the chartership standard. In my organisation at that time there was limited funding available for external training and I ended up funding some of the risk assessment workshops that now enhance my CV.

I worked in a secure hospital environment with offenders who have a learning disability. I completed assessment and intervention work with core client groups such as sex offenders, violent offenders and fire-setters. Working with offenders with a learning disability inspired me to train as an intermediary with the criminal justice system and I now facilitate communication between the police, the courts and adult witnesses and suspects with a learning disability. This work is very rewarding and has opened my eyes wide to the judicial system.

Chapter 3: What type of work does a forensic psychologist do?

Some people get confused by the word *forensic* and associate the term with working in scientific laboratories using microscopes to analyse exhibits from scenes of crime. As you probably know that is not the function of the forensic psychologist and you would be better seeking information about pathology or related fields if you are interested in that area of practice. Many people seem to associate the work of a forensic psychologist with the criminal justice system; it should be noted that forensic psychologists could also work in the field of civil law, for example, assessing the cognitive functioning of someone detained in a secure hospital under civil sections of the Mental Health Act. Forensic psychologists may also carry out assessments for the family courts. The term forensic psychologist really means the application of psychological theory and practice to the legal system. Psychologists may be employed as researchers and lecturers at universities or as applied practitioners in the field. Some psychologists may even work in split posts dividing their time between research and applied practice.

Most forensic psychologists however do commence their training in the criminal justice system, working in the prison service or in secure hospitals. The work is likely to entail meeting offenders on a 1:1 basis or in a group scenario and carrying out psychological assessments and treatment interventions. Psychologists also assess offenders for the risk that they pose both within the location that they are incarcerated in and for the risk that they pose if they were to be transferred to less secure accommodation. The forensic psychologist is likely to work with offenders with backgrounds in the broad categories of violence, sexual offending and fire-setting. The nature of this work can be distressing, as you will be attempting to find out what motivates these individuals to offend and to help them find ways to manage their risk of re-offending. This will undoubtedly involve taking a full case history and reading accounts of the offending behaviour. Are you suited to this kind of work? I recall the first time that I interviewed a lifer and I was aware that I was looking at the offender's hands; the hands that had murdered someone many years previously. Some offenders can be highly manipulative and will attempt to engage you in discussing the details of the offence behaviour as they gain further satisfaction from re-living the experience. You will, of course, be supervised by a qualified psychologist as you begin to engage in this work.

As a qualified psychologist you may choose to work in many other areas of the criminal justice system. For example, forensic psychologists may work with families in the community who have been identified as likely to end up in the criminal justice system if they are not offered a suitable intervention. Some psychologists may specialise in consultancy to the police service or act as hostage negotiators or experts in profiling offenders. There are many options once qualified. Indeed there are some opportunities, although rare, to undertake your training outside of the prison service or hospitals by identifying a forensic psychologist in private practice who is willing to supervise you.

Forensic psychologists are encouraged to be research-practitioners and may be tasked with carrying out psychological research about the people or the environment where they work. Examples of such research may include ways to reduce the occurrence of bullying in the establishment or how to reduce the risk of suicide and self-harming behaviour. The psychologist is also expected to take an active role in training members of staff about psychological theories and processes. For example I trained nursing staff and care workers about personality disorders and how 'splitting' could occur both within teams and across teams. The psychologist works in collaboration with a wider professional network which depending on where you work may include prison officers, probation officers, nursing staff, social workers, occupational therapists to name but a few. As a psychologist it will be expected that you can develop excellent report writing skills and that in time you will develop to be a competent and confident speaker at hearings and as a trainer. Once again, your supervisor should support you as you develop in these key areas of practice.

There are also opportunities in the long term of working independently as a psychologist. Many experienced forensic psychologists have left the prison service and have set up as independent practitioners specialising for example in the writing of risk assessment reports for parole board hearings. Indeed this is currently the area within which I practise and I frequently complete risk assessments of lifers and other prisoners who are seeking progressive moves to open prison conditions or to release on licence into the community.

Chapter 4: How do you train to become a forensic psychologist?

I would strongly urge you to frequently visit the website of the British Psychological Society (BPS) in order to keep up to date with the changing nature of the training requirements to become a forensic psychologist. I am writing this book at a time when the Health & Care Professionals Council (HCPC) has taken over the regulation of applied psychologists. You need to explore the role that the HCPC plays in regulating applied psychologists. I have included the addresses for the BPS and the HCPC at the end of this book. Nowadays it is possible to practise as a registered psychologist without being chartered through the BPS.

You will find the current main system of training fully outlined in the BPS Candidate Handbook *Qualification in Forensic Psychology Stage 2* (2011). This manual is available on the BPS website. I will however give you a brief overview of the system to keep you involved until you access the current candidate handbook.

Firstly, by now you will hopefully have attained or be hoping to gain a good honours degree (at least a 2:2 but hopefully a 2:1 or a First) in a psychology degree, which will give you the graduate basis for registration (GBR) with the BPS. (GBR has been renamed as GBC). The BPS website can assist you if you are unsure whether your degree qualifies. (I have recently been contacted by a graduate in Criminology who has applied for a non-accredited MSc and yet wonders why rejection letters keep arriving on her doorstop for psychology jobs that she has applied for with the prison service. It would appear that no-one has told this individual that she can *never* become a registered applied psychologist without meeting the basic requirements. To start with her undergraduate degree does not have GBC.) If you already hold an accredited MSc you will also hopefully have secured a job (or intend to get a job) in an environment such as a prison or a secure hospital which employs chartered psychologists who are registered as Forensic Psychologists with the HCPC. The DFP candidate handbook does state that it is possible to train in other environments though such as policing or probation. For most people though your first paid job is likely to be that of a psychological assistant or an assistant psychologist and even to get that post you are likely to have already worked in a healthcare setting or completed some voluntary work. I have had several graduates with a 2:1 degree in psychology email me and express feelings of disillusionment because they cannot secure a trainee position immediately on graduation. To obtain a trainee post that quickly, even when in possession of an MSc in Forensic Psychology, would be very lucky and extremely rare.

I will outline later in the book the various routes that some trainees have taken in order to kick-start their career. Competition is usually fierce for assistant and trainee jobs. You will be competing against other graduates who usually will have included on the application form copious details of what they have learned from their voluntary and paid employment in relevant fields. Do not be complacent.

If you already have an accredited MSc and are employed in a suitable forensic setting you may be able to apply to commence Stage 2 of the Qualification in Forensic Psychology and this consists of *at least* two years full time employment (or equivalent part-time) which has been supervised by a qualified psychologist. (The Annual DFP

Survey 2010-2011(Forensic Update, October 2012) found that In-Training members had been enrolled on the Qualification in Forensic Psychology for an average of three years, with a range between one and nine years. That means that at least one candidate has been in-training for a nine year period). You will need to apply for Conditional Registration with the British Psychological Society. Once you are conditionally registered you can commence the Practice Dimension, Stage 2, of the Qualification where you will eventually produce four separate portfolios of written evidence to demonstrate your competence in the four core roles of conducting applications and interventions, research, communicating with other professionals and training other professionals. Examples of this portfolio work are provided later in this book from a couple of the contributors.

Importantly, the BPS stipulates the time limits that you must work within and so you must seek support with your supervisor at all stages of planning. I must reiterate that I have only provided an overview in this chapter of the current main route of getting qualified and I urge you to check out the appropriate pages on the website (BPS & HCPC) at the time you begin to read this book.

At the time of publication (January 2013) I have been made aware that there is an alternative route (Cardiff Metropolitan University) of qualifying to work as a forensic psychologist registered with the HCPC, but not chartered with the BPS. This route is a Post Graduate Diploma Forensic Psychology Practitioner Programme and is placement based. It currently has students in Wales, England and Scotland and intends to enrol students from Northern Ireland soon. There are also professional doctorate programmes run by the Universities of Nottingham and Birmingham that include the Stage 2 element of training as part of the doctorate and on completion you would be registered with the HCPC and Chartered with the BPS. There might also be an opportunity to take the "top up" route if you already hold an accredited MSc degree.

It is therefore really important that you consider from the outset what suits you in terms of your location, training preference, financial limitations and ultimately which bodies you wish to be registered with when you have completed your training.

Chapter 5: Alternative career choices

There are a number other divisions in the BPS in addition to the Division of Forensic Psychology and I firstly want to offer a brief introduction to their names and secondly, to inform you that many psychologists from the other applied divisions may work in a forensic environment. I appreciate that this information may be confusing to you but it is really important that I make you aware of this fact so that you can explore from the outset the alternative careers that you can have as a psychologist which will require different training routes should you choose to follow one of them. I make this comment because I know that many potential forensic psychologists are totally unaware that many clinical and counselling psychologists specialise in the forensic field after qualifying and I would ask you this question: Have you even considered the other Divisions within the BPS before heading straight into an MSc in forensic psychology?

I was recently contacted by a solicitor who wanted to instruct me as an expert witness in a case where the defendant was alleging that they acted under duress committing a crime due to the trauma they had suffered as a victim in a previous violent incident. This was outside my area of skill and expertise and may be better suited to a clinical psychologist who specialises in post-traumatic stress disorder or a forensic psychologist who has specialised in this area after initial training. I use the case as an example to illustrate that just because a case goes to the criminal court does not mean that the forensic psychologist is the best person to take it.

When I was researching this book one qualified psychologist wrote the following email to me which inspired me to include this information in the book:

There are quite a lot of psychologists who work in the forensic arena that are not Chartered Forensic Psychologists, and nor will ever be. I am a chartered Counselling Psychologist by background, and derive two-thirds of my income from forensic psychology

The other divisions of the BPS are called:

Division of Clinical Psychology
Division of Counselling Psychology
Division of Educational and Child Psychology (& Scottish Division of Educational Psychology)
Division of Health psychology
Division of Neuropsychology
Division of Occupational Psychology
Division of Sport and Exercise Psychology
Division for Teachers and Researchers in Psychology

In the time that I have worked in a secure hospital I have had the benefit of working with applied psychologists from the divisions of clinical, counselling and forensic psychology. You may wish to read about a debate that was aired in the BPS publication *Psychologist* (December 2008, February & March 2009) that centres on the confusion that seems to have arisen when some jobs are advertised for clinically or forensic trained psychologists.

Many people graduating with a psychology degree will not train to be psychologists. Again, without wishing to turn you away from a career in forensic psychology (a career which I find very rewarding), I want to remind you that there are a number of other careers where you could meet forensic clients without training as a psychologist. For example, you may consider a career with the prison service, the probation service or a career as a nurse working in a forensic unit. Of course you could also consider working for a Youth Offending Team or maybe the police service. Have you considered fraud investigation? What about substance misuse agencies? Do you know what crime analysts do?

Did you know that some probation officers and prison officers choose to specialise as facilitators on offending behaviour programmes in HM Prison Service or in the community? Is that a role that would suit you?

Question:

How does the role of a forensic psychologist differ from that of a probation officer?

Chapter 6: Survey of in-training members

In 2009 I conducted a small survey amongst forensic psychologists in training (i.e. these were not assistant psychologists or care workers but had achieved posts with the title Forensic Psychologist in training) and I will present some of the findings below. I accept that there are methodological issues with this sample and I am not suggesting that it is representative of all trainees' experiences. Some of the comments may seem negative but it would be pointless if I were to rattle off a list that suggested that trainees never had any concerns. I must inform you that it appears that the training route has settled down a bit since 2009 and that the following comments may not be as relevant today (2013) as they were when I collected the data. Undoubtedly though, these qualitative data comments do raise issues that you may wish to consider.

Survey Results
You can supplement these findings by also looking at the published results of an official survey completed by the Division of Forensic Psychology in 2008 (BPS website).

Trainee Forensic Psychologists Responses to Questionnaire Survey

Nineteen trainees responded to the questionnaire which was made available on the website www.traineeforensicpsychologist.com

Demographics:

The sample comprised of the following people:18 females and 1 male

Age Range: 21- 25: 3 (two of whom were aged 25 and the other aged 24)
            26-30: 12
            31-40: 4
            41+: 0

What is quite striking about this small sample is the number of participants who are aged over 25. This might take some of the pressure off newly qualified graduates who assume that they must gain employment immediately as a trainee.

Current Employment: 15 participants were employed by HM Prison Service and the remaining 4 work in the forensic hospital sector.

All respondents were on the Diploma route to qualification as a chartered psychologist (This route has subsequently changed and candidates embarking on the training route will now need to complete an MSc in order to satisfy the requirements of Stage 1 of the training).

Trainees had been conditionally registered with the British Psychological Society for an average of two years with a range between eleven months and five years.

Most respondents hoped that they would be in the role of supervised trainees and therefore conditionally registered for a maximum period of three to four years although one respondent indicated 6 years+, one stated "forever" and another stated "no idea".

Seventeen out of the 19 respondents indicated that they already held an MSc degree in forensic psychology, and out of these eight respondents held the MSc prior to obtaining their post as a trainee forensic psychologist.

Ten respondents who already have an MSc in Forensic Psychology indicated that they had self-funded their postgraduate study whereas six respondents indicated that HM Prison Service funded theirs.

Previous work as an assistant:

I asked how many of the respondents had held a post as a Psychological Assistant (Prison Service) or Assistant Psychologist (Healthcare) prior to obtaining their post as a trainee.

Fourteen out of the 18 respondents had previously held posts as assistants.

Of these 14, the average length of time spent working in an assistant post was 16 months, with a range of a few weeks to three years.

Number of applications made for trainee posts before being successful:

The average number of applications made for trainee posts was two per person with a range of between one and six applications, with 10 respondents gaining a trainee place in the establishment where they had held an assistant post. One trainee reports that a post was actually created for her within her establishment when she was offered posts elsewhere. This really does show the importance of getting your foot in the door as an assistant and showing them what you can do.

Other relevant previous work experiences:

Trainees listed the following types of relevant work experience that they had prior to obtaining a job as a trainee forensic psychologist; you can note the familiar themes emerging of voluntary work, youth work and health care work

Drugs work, probation work & voluntary work with a forensic population
Two and a half years working as an offending behaviour and groupwork specialist with persistent and prolific young offenders
Twelve months as a learning support assistant at a young offender's institute
Working for a youth offending team
Worked in voluntary sector: Victim support SACRO
Eighteen months with youth offending team

9 months as a health care assistant and three years' part-time work with MIND as an appropriate adult
Probation service officer
Volunteer at a youth offending team
One year as a Health Care assistant in a secure unit
Psychological assistant and programmes work
Salesman and a trainer
SACRO
Admin officer in a prison; mentor for young offenders
Volunteer post with HM Prison Service
Research assistant whilst at university

The issues that trainees see as challenges with their training programme:

It is clear from the consistency of the comments that trainees feel that they just don't have enough time in the working week to meet their employer's needs and those of the chartership role.

It is also clear that although trainees are in trainee posts there is not enough variety in many posts to allow the trainee to achieve the core roles necessary for chartership

Pay- too low for too long which restricts many things such as getting a mortgage and having a family
Need to spend a lot of your private time doing the work towards chartership
Limited role in our jobs is not broad enough to gain enough experience to meet all the competencies
Lots of trainees get stuck doing programmes such as sex offender treatment- we don't get the opportunity to meet the other core roles
Not always possible to get the scope of work within one department
Poor work / life balance
The conflict between the chartership requirements and the needs of working for the prison service
No time to maintain the practice diary
Limited supervision available
Fitting in the time to undertake exemplars an write up reports whilst also holding down a full-time job with a full caseload
Cost of supervision as well as BPS fees
Constant conflict between organisational requirements and developmental (Chartership) requirements
Lack of support can lead to a loss of motivation
Lack of time; tutoring full-time on a programme means that I have no time for anything else
Finding enough time to complete chartership work, therefore, practice diaries and core roles
Not enough support and guidance regarding what needs to be done; no support with fees

I asked what advice the current trainees would give to those hoping to embark on a career in forensic psychology:

Don't think that it is easy to complete chartership; it takes a lot of extra time
Stay focused on your goal
Be organised throughout
Make sure that you really go through the guidance before starting and get as much experience as you can in the forensic field
Allow a lot of time. Try to avoid trainee roles that involve programmes work, as you are likely to find it really difficult to meet the chartership rules with regards to breadth of experience
Don't do it! Take the clinical psychology route to training!
Keep practice diary and supervision log up to date
Keep a written record of everything (conversations, meetings etc)
Be prepared to work on your chartership in addition to your working hours
Complete your MSc whilst working within a prison to consolidate your learning
Be confident of your abilities and be committed to work outside of work
Time management skills and organisational skills are crucial
Network with other trainees
Make sure this is definitely what you want to do because it takes a lot to stay motivated at the challenging times
Make sure you have a good supervisor; it's crucial
Don't do it unless you are clear about the expectations
Consider an alternative career such as with the probation service
Consider what you enjoy about this field because some prisons and secure hospitals can offer you different experiences
Take some time to speak to trainees first before you commit to the training.
Start young when you can afford the time and you don't want to start a family
Be prepared to give up your weekends and evenings
Try to make the most of work opportunities for work experience and volunteering in areas such as children, mental health, care work etc.

I asked trainees what one thing they would do differently if they were starting out again:

I wouldn't have started the forensic training route
I would have considered a doctorate programme because that would guarantee me chartership after three years
Do my MSc straight after my degree, rather than getting experience
Maybe do my MSc through the prison service
Talk to trainees to get a better idea of what I am committing to
Do my practice diary and supervision log regularly, and keep accurate written records
Get more work experience, as I would have got a job sooner as I temped for a year after doing my MSc before getting a job as a psychological assistant
Ensure that my practice diary entries are made at least weekly
I would take more care with my selection of various supervisors

Only undertake work, which would take me through chartership
Do my MSc straight after university- then I would be a senior chartered psychologist by now
Seek wider experience than the prison service can offer me
Gain some experience as a trainee before registering for Stage 2
Start younger or not at all

Now, most importantly, I asked the trainees what they really enjoyed about their job as a trainee forensic psychologist and received the following positive responses:

The people; delivering programmes; learning and training
Facilitating groups to both staff and prisoners is the most enjoyable part of my job; it is exciting and different every day. Job satisfaction is good when you know you have facilitated change in a client
Variety of work; working with challenging people
Always learning new ways of dealing with problems
Having various tools of intervention and detailed knowledge that helps promote work that really targets area of need
Time allowed to work on sex offender treatment programme
The challenge
Working with prisoners and contributing to risk assessments
Seeing progress in clients and hearing them acknowledge my role in that
Working with offenders and writing risk assessments
The learning experience; although it has been tough and very frustrating at times, by going through the process and being near the end, I feel ready to take on the role as a qualified psychologist
The range of tasks the constant learning and challenges
The diversity of people that I work with, both clients and colleagues
Opportunity to think and to use my initiative
The support from my colleagues
I love my job; it is very challenging, varied and rewarding
I enjoy all aspects of my work, including working with patients (conducting assessments, delivering interventions) and working with other members of staff.
The opportunity to work with prisoners; the variety of work
I am constantly challenged both intellectually and personally
I can see how my work effects changes in people
Working with patients and conducting psychological therapies
Interesting, challenging work; no two days are the same. Unpredictable clients, varied work
Working with a wide range of complex needs and being able to provide helpful support and treatment
Seeing progress in a patient whom you have helped them achieve is a brilliant sense of achievement

In the following chapters (**Part 2**) you will be offered the opportunity to read qualitative accounts provided by a number of psychologists who are qualified or who are forensic psychologists-in-training. You can also read the accounts of two people who commenced the training route but who chose to leave it before getting qualified. I have given the writers the choice of being named in this book or remaining anonymous and some have chosen the latter option. For ease of reading I have allocated pseudonyms to those who wish to remain anonymous and I randomly selected these pseudonyms from the names of authors who have had academic articles published in a recent psychology journal.

In the following chapter we hear from Marilyn who describes how she qualified by completing her training in a hospital setting. Then Sally provides an account of her experiences of training within HM Prison Service and independently and she describes the advantages of her chosen route.

Part 2

Chapter 7 – Accounts from successful trainees

Marilyn Sher *successfully completed the training route in a remarkably quick time. In this account she tells us how she managed this achievement. Since qualifying as a forensic psychologist Marilyn has subsequently gained dual chartership as a clinical psychologist. This account emerged from an audio-recorded interview that I conducted with Marilyn and the presentation style is of an edited interview transcript. I hope that this different approach allows for an informal chatty approach and I think that it allows for natural humour to shine through.*

I did my undergraduate degree abroad - at the time by correspondence because I had moved out of home pretty young and so was working. So it was one of those times, working as a book-keeper in-between, trying to get through undergraduate psychology, and then as soon as I finished it, that's when I came to England. But they wouldn't accept my degree over here. So they (the British Psychological Society) wanted me to do a conversion course, which I did at Westminster University, which was a graduate diploma in psychology. And I did one of the elective modules in forensic psychology. But my interest had predated that. When I was a little kid I was one of those children that was quite fascinated with all the blood and gore and stuff and knew I wanted to understand why people did these things and work in that field and I wanted to do psychology but I used to say to my parents, "I want to study psychology but I don't want to see just clients with depression" and that was my kind of take on things, on the clinical aspect. I think a clinical psychologist would probably correct me right now if they heard that. But that was my naïve take on things at the time. And so I've always known that I had an interest in the forensic aspect of things and I wanted to do forensic psychology, but my home country didn't offer such a thing, so I knew I needed to look elsewhere for a course. I was aware there were courses in the UK, and when I commenced my postgraduate diploma, that's when I really started looking into it more. When I completed the postgraduate diploma I went to the University of Surrey and did my Masters.

I found that to be another one of those stressful experiences because at the time there were only four Universities that did the forensic Masters Degree. Surrey was considered the place to go if you went and it was one of those awful experiences where there were like four hundred applicants for about 20 places; they interviewed eighty of us; I got an interview and left there in tears after all these fantastic impressive people were there going on about all this experience that they had beforehand and thinking I haven't got a chance in hell, but yet got on the course somehow. The only work experience I had up to that point had been working as an appropriate adult as a volunteer for Mind on the weekends for a couple years beforehand. That was the extent of my experience.

The MSc was phenomenal. I loved the Surrey MSc, it was very hands-on. We had good links with a High Secure Hospital; I did my dissertation there; the course was exactly what I wanted. There was a heavy emphasis on mental health as well as the investigative side of forensic psychology which interests me and I've started a PhD now, which is quite different to what I'm doing here, day to day. But going back again, whilst on the MSc I think I still had a very naive view of well, I'm going to walk off this MSc and you know, practice now, I'm going to be qualified you know, and I think I was only about half way through, and I don't quite know how I got that far without quite realising what was still involved, that someone on my course mentioned that this is only Stage One of the qualification process. It was at that point I think that the majority of us on the course became aware of the process and I think we should all have been informed much earlier of the exact details of the route to qualification. I think the (BPS) diploma route was also still quite new; before all the changes I think previously you could charter just by having worked in the field for a few years and fill in a form. So I think that's part of why there was this confusion and it was a big shock for a lot of us to find out how far we had to go to get qualified. I think I finished the MSc degree in 2004.

Yes, so I'm pretty sure that it was June 2004 when we finished. So it was "hit panic stations" [laughter] and I'd still no psychology experience at that point besides working for Mind. Oh yes, I remember how it happened; I had to go to the High Secure Hospital to do an induction because I was going to do my research there and I had to go through the basic induction in order to gain access to the hospital to go and do my research. It was on that induction that I met a girl who'd also done a forensic MSc at some point and she was getting work experience, prior to becoming an assistant psychologist, through being a Health Care Assistant at the hospital; and she made a suggestion to me, said it'll give you the experience you need to get an AP (Assistant psychologist) post. I applied to the hospital for a Health Care Assistant job and worked there for nine months. I started before my MSc was complete; I think I started in the March and worked there for nine months and it was after that I got my first assistant post here at the hospital.

I'll tell you more about working at the High Secure hospital. I was lucky with that because I worked on a really settled ward, whereas some of my friends ended up on some very high intensive wards. Whereas mine was rehab, a lot of them (patients) had been there for a long time or were on their way out. So I was pretty lucky in that respect because it was quite a shock as well having no experience, never even set foot in a hospital or secure environment like that before, to see what it was. But I absolutely loved it. My job really involved doing the nursing assistant work. So you'd work shifts, do the radio, escorting patients around, doing security checks, giving meals, and just being a kind of a presence there and obviously respond and if there's incidents and being involved in restraints and stuff. So it was really good in two respects; it gave me some kind of entry to that environment but also gave me the experience of what it was like for the nursing staff and that's one of those things that have been in my favour all along, in my psychology training and career. Because I'm sure as you know, one of our biggest challenges working in a mental health setting is working collaboratively with nursing staff and being able to turn around and say 'yes, I have done some work on the shop floor, I've done my nightshifts" you know, "I've been there on shifts and working with patients one to one like that all the time. I know where you're coming from!" And it gives you that point, that extra point. So, I worked there for nine months.

At that point I think a lot of our lectures were coming to an end and we were working really very much on our dissertations at that time. I was able to balance the academic side with working. The nice thing about the health care assistant work is it's the kind of stuff that you go in, do your shift and leave. It's not like work now where you've you know, you've got deadlines and things that you have to do after hours. Your work was entirely what you did on the shift. There was nothing you could take home with you. So when you weren't on shift that was perfect for me to do my MSc stuff. Again, it's not very psychologically intensive, the health care assistant work. So you didn't come off feeling drained either. In a sense, it was actually the perfect kind of work to do whilst doing my MSc, because I didn't find it draining, either physically or emotionally. But then I suppose also I was on a less challenging ward.

You can get a health care assistant job with virtually no experience. Health Care Assistant posts are graded as A, B and C grades; "A" being the lowest grade, "C" being the highest health care assistant grade; with the psychology degree or background, you automatically come in as a "B" grade. But "A" grades come from all walks of life. We've got some here at this hospital that had a complete career change and then would come in as "A" grades. What's nice about it is you don't need any previous experience to get you into that. Yet the role is very good at helping you get an assistant post afterwards.

If people asked me now "what is the first step to getting into the forensic psychology field?" I would say start as a health care assistant, even if it's just for a relatively short period of time. I mean I was lucky because I'd been applying for assistant posts for ages and was dealing with all that awful feeling of being rejected left, right and centre and not even making it to interview. But I still got an assistant post very quickly compared to some of my friends. Some of them were doing health care assistant work for a couple of years before they got an assistant post. I suppose it's about timing and how you are at interviews and opportunities and things like that. But yes, I did get my post quite quickly, so I was lucky. We've talked a little bit about the inevitable rejection letters that you get when you're applying for AP posts and I think that is the reality for everyone; you just have to cope with it. There's nothing you can do; everyone goes through that and even once you've had your first AP post, you can go through the process of a large number of rejections again when trying to get into your second one.

The feedback from prospective employers is not always helpful; sometimes you hear nothing. I'm still waiting to see if I got one post as an assistant in the South. I haven't heard yet. [Laughter] It's a running joke. I still don't know if I got the job. I think there are so many people who apply for these jobs; well if you get rejected on application, you just heard nothing very often. Sometimes you wouldn't even get a letter to say you didn't get an interview. And in terms of interviews, the feedback would be so sketchy that it was like worthless. Nowadays, I know that when we advertise a vacancy for an assistant psychologist post we may get around one hundred and fifty applications. That is tough competition. We don't advertise for trainee forensic psychologists; usually those are people who come in as assistants and at some point if people are happy with them and they're really motivated they can progress when a trainee post comes up.

My first job actually working as an assistant psychologist was working with older adults, males, who were on a medium secure unit. I covered two wards at the time. One ward, which was a medium secure ward, a lot of the men were ex-high security patients who were still very dangerous and not suitable for release and were kind of coming in to live the rest of their life until old age in a secure environment. But they needed to come into medium security because they were becoming vulnerable in high security. The other ward was more for people with challenging behaviour because they had developed conditions like dementia and things had deteriorated for them. So, again I was in one of those lucky situations; I came in as an assistant and the perception from the qualified psychologists was that I was a clinical assistant, with some forensic interest and I was okay to go with that. Your first Assistant Psychology post, you do what they tell you, you know; you don't be picky [laughter]. But I was exceptionally lucky again and three months into the job a forensic psychologist who'd always worked in the prisons joined us; she'd been one of the managers there but decided to come and work on the hospital wards as a qualified psychologist. I can be a real pain in the butt and from the day that she arrived I nagged and nagged and nagged her; 'please let me do my Chartership through you, please will you supervise me?' She was lovely and she said yes. I had to pay all my fees myself, but the management were happy for her to use her time during the working hours to do the necessary supervision, and for me to do some of my exemplar work. This was very, very new for both of us, because she hadn't obtained her Chartership on the new route and she'd never supervised anyone doing that route. I didn't know anybody else that was doing it and so it was a case of getting hold of the Red Book (Guidelines) and study it from page one to the next. And so yes, about six or seven months into my first Assistant Psychologist post I signed up for the Chartership training.

Technically, at that time I didn't change my title to Trainee Forensic Psychologist; they kept me initially as an Assistant Psychologist and then a bit later on the hospital upgraded me to a trainee and I was the first Trainee Forensic Psychologist in the whole hospital. They'd never done that before. Now suffice to say, I've started a trend and there are quite a few trainees [laughter]... I guess because I was the first one in the hospital, I think they were all quite sceptical and nervous about the whole thing. Whereas now, it's done a lot, the service knows about the process and the trainees get study days off and support for their research and exemplars and also money towards CPD. So there has been quite a bit of change since I started it all. I was unfortunately the guinea pig, and because of that I was just a nag, it was awful. But it got me where I wanted to be.

You have to be so motivated and just be in people's faces until they just get so sick and tired of saying "no" they just cave in and say "okay". [Laughter] You have to be and I just want to say this now, is that we had a few people contact me along the way and say "we're interested in doing forensic psychology, what do you think...?" you know, blah blah, and my first piece of advice to them is you have to be sure and passionate about it, because if you're not passionate and you're not sure about wanting to do it, don't, because it is, it's a challenge, it's a nightmare, you're going to go through times you just want to give up and unless you've got that drive and perseverance to push through, it's not going to happen, and so don't waste your time beforehand. I mean I think part of it I think [laughter] was I just finished and was exhausted and thought it was a really arduous task. But that would still be my advice; unless you're passionate about it, don't even go there! And it can be expensive. It took me two and a half years of supervised practice. I did it in record time though.

Those two and a half years I can honestly say did nearly kill me and I went through a supervisor change as well. My first supervisor was phenomenal, although she was very new to everything, she was very, very pernickety and very particular about how she wanted things done, and she had a lot of experience with male offenders, in terms of violent and sexual offence histories. That was my particular area of interest and she really gave me that very basic... how do I put it... she set the standard in terms of what type of work I needed to be producing from the beginning, and to this day I still make her giggle and get all embarrassed. I say "if it wasn't for you I wouldn't be the psychologist I am today!" And she ended up only supervising me for six months because eventually she got sick of the whole thing and said "oh hell, I want to go back to studying" and she went and did her clinical (psychology) training and she went on the actual clinical course and did it like that. So, anyway, she couldn't supervise me anymore and I went on the BPS website and had a look at which forensic psychologists were in the area and started my [laughter] badgering again. But I was really, really lucky because there was a Principal forensic psychologist who was, at that time... well we had two forensic psychologists in the hospital; one in the men's service who I approached; she said she was too busy to take me. I cried big crocodile tears and it still didn't warm her heart. [Laughter] She's a good friend today, so she won't mind me saying that. And then another one who was working in our service in the South East who again had never supervised anyone on the new route but she was a lovely woman who was looking to develop her skills in the area and agreed to supervise me. The challenge here was that instead of now having face-to-face supervision, this was supervision by email and telephone. And there's a big difference to kind of get used to this method of supervision. But it's doable and sometimes you're in that position where you have to do that because you might not have someone who can supervise you within your work environment and so you have to look at what options are available and it was okay. It wasn't ideal, but it was okay. And that kind of got me through. In terms of how we did it in two and a half years, it was a bit of hit and miss.

Stage two of the Chartership training was to me those awful four key roles [laughter] and two examples (called Exemplars) of each. And it was slightly different to how it is now, in that you could send in as you finished one exemplar, you could submit it to the BPS for marking. Whereas, now, as far as I'm aware, you have to do both exemplars per key role and submit them together. I liked the old route because if you weren't doing what they were hoping you would, you could learn from your mistakes on the first one and do your best to pass the second one. As I say, it when I was doing my first exemplar, I sat there with this Red Book (Guidelines), which did seem to have a hell of a lot of detail in terms of what they were looking for. So that was one of the things that I was a bit confused about; I couldn't quite understand why some of my peers were saying they didn't know what the BPS wanted from you. That's what I thought initially. Why do people not know what the BPS wants from you, because there's lots of detail about what they expect you to achieve in an exemplar. And so when I was writing my first one I was pretty anxious but I did a very comprehensive one and made sure that I followed each of the criteria that they were listing in the Red Book and if I hadn't covered an area, I explained in detail why I hadn't. This culminated in reflective reports that were of ridiculous length. I'm trying to remember... I think they on average used to be between 20 and 30 pages of A4. I got some very good feedback. I think they used a few of my reflective reports for some of the training for supervisors. Yet other colleagues of mine were getting exemplars sent back and said they were too long; their reflective reports. So I think that's where some of the problems were coming in, that there seemed to be inconsistency in the marking.

Basically what you would need to do was you'd send to the Chief Supervisor a plan of what you wanted to do for a particular exemplar and stipulate how you would go about doing that piece of work and get that approved. In terms of how you submitted the work, I used to put my exemplars together using a reflective report as the bulk piece and then would add supplementary materials on to evidence how I achieved each of the criteria in an appendix. And then I would include a supervisor log and practice diary as well, as separate documents. But I always used the reflective report as a way to draw all the material together, because it just kind of made sense to me; you've got to talk these people through exactly what you've done in the most coherent way possible and I would use colour and referencing so that they knew exactly what material to go to for what. So I made it very, very easy for the person sitting there marking my exemplar to see what I was talking about and which piece of material was evidence for which parts of the exemplar. So, in this reflective report, obviously it was talking through my process and what work I had done, but at the same time I was taking the opportunity to reflect on my practice, because they put so much emphasis on reflection.

So, for example, Core Role 1, I'm trying to think now how I did it... Well, the first one I did was on the older adults division. Yes, that one was assessment and intervention. So yes, I had four patients that I did individual work with on the older adults division and so I took them through the whole initial assessment processes; the interventions I identified and that formed part of the first example. So there were four examples for the first submission of one to one work on a few different areas. I think one was anger management, one was like sex education, and one was purely a behavioural intervention because there was challenging behaviour. I can't remember what the last one was... I think it was similar, quite a behavioural type program. It was a good way to work as I was able to demonstrate a breath of experience, which is a main requirement.

Then the second exemplar for that core role was on the adolescent service where I delivered a group aggression replacement training programme, and so it was six adolescents on that group and it was about the pre-assessment, delivering the group, and then post-group evaluation.

Core Role Two; that is the one about research. You're allowed to draw on one of your other key roles, on occasion, and extend that further for the research exemplars. So for that one I took the aggression replacement training group that I'd done with the adolescents, re-delivered it because our service is split into two; so we've got one 'division' which is adolescents with emerging personality disorder and mental health difficulties and then a different "division" which is developmental disability, learning disability and autism. So I delivered the group again and then wrote up a paper comparing the two groups and just describing the processes, so kind of piggy-backed off some of the work I'd done already which was a good idea because it reduced a bit of the work I had to do. And then for the second exemplar for this core role I did an evaluation of community meetings on the adolescent service and observed some community meetings, I did some interviews and then I got the patients to do the group environment scale as well to evaluate the community meeting. You've got to be really careful with obtaining the correct ethics approval on doing this type of research and may often have to gain approval from the NHS ethics committee as well as from the BPS. You cannot afford to make mistakes with ethics.

On the first piece of research the assessors hadn't passed me; initially, they gave me a conditional pass, as they weren't happy with the fact that I had used non-parametric statistics on my sample. They felt the sample was too small to do any actual statistics on; I had 12 patients, six and six, for that one and I picked non-parametric. And they said it would have been better to have done a series of single case studies. So they gave me a conditional pass and then I had to do... What I did was I did some reflection on why I had chosen the non-parametric statistics, how a series of single cases would've been better, and I provided one example of a single case, and submitted that back and they passed it.

Now, Key Role Three; that was the "fluffy" one. That was quite a difficult one, as it is about consultation. It is a very hard one I suppose for people in a trainee position. The first exemplar for this one, again was an older adult service and I think that centred, yes, that centred around doing reports and feeding those reports back within my job role, so that's like the ward rounds, Care Programme Approach meetings (CPA), things like that. I also included in there that I had been invited with an external psychiatrist to go and present one of the cases at a "grand round" at another psychiatric hospital. Also, I wrote an informal paper for a publication that specialises in the treatment of sex offenders about risk assessing older adults and the complications. I also did a presentation at the Division of Forensic Psychology (DFP) annual conference. So it was quite a variety of work.

Just to explain some of those meetings that I attended. The Care Program Approach meetings; those are meetings where the whole clinical team get together, the patient themselves and any external people who are involved and you review that patient every six months in terms of what's being going on in those six months and any progress or any deterioration and what your plans are for the next review period. So I presented my psychology reports about patients to professionals such as psychiatrists, social workers, occupational therapists and nurses. I had to be confident to explain my psychological findings and to answer any questions about my work. I also had to be able to speak to the patient and the family about the report; so you really need to be adaptable with your approach as a psychologist. I remember the first time I had to attend one of these meetings. My notes were shaking. My face was red [Laughter] It's quite, you know, there's a lot of practitioners there from a lot of professional backgrounds. It can be very intimidating.

Then I mentioned the annual conference by the Division of Forensic Psychology (DFP). It's a good opportunity I suppose to get yourself out there and get over your fear of public speaking; and that kind of piggy-backed off the work that I was doing; I focused that exemplar on the older adult work that I was doing for that DFP presentation; it was on the complications of risk assessing older adults because our risk assessment tools aren't specifically designed for them and very often with that client group you'd have individuals who've had a completely "normal" stable life and suddenly at the age of 76 turned around and murdered their wife. So your usual risk assessments are not going to give you any indication something's going to happen or happen again in the future. So that's what that exemplar focused on. So, I've told you now about speaking at clinical meetings and public speaking at a conference. Then there was the attendance at the famous psychiatric hospital in London. I was invited to go and present my psychology data there. Again, absolutely a terrifying experience and anyone who's been to one of those *grand rounds*, you know how some professionals are just out there to attempt to discredit you and that's their main intention! [Laughter]

I was actually making these presentations quite early on in my training. I was working on the older adult service; I think I worked there for nine months as a trainee, before I then started moving on to the adolescent service. So it was pretty early on. It was definitely the earlier stages of my Chartership [laughter] and I still don't know how I did it. But you do these things and that's the thing again, you have to be so driven and just put your fears aside, even if it means taking a shot of alcohol just before [laughter] to calm the nerves, or a bunch of Kalms meds from the chemist, you just do what you need to do. [Laughter] Oh the other core role three exemplar I think was from my work on the adolescent service; that was quite a simple one actually because I was still working on the older adult service and I again was one of those who nagged, bribed, pleaded the clinical psychologist in the adolescent service to please let me volunteer for half a day a week, because she didn't want to take me on as an assistant, didn't know me, didn't think I'd be any good [laughter] at the time and agreed to let me come and do some half day voluntary stuff and I did six risk assessments on six different patients and presented those at the CPA meetings and to the ward based staff at away days. And that was the second exemplar! So even when I was in post as a trainee forensic psychologist I was still doing voluntary work on half a day to get the breadth of experience I needed! It paid off though, as that gave the clinical psychologist the opportunity to see my work and she subsequently gave me a job. [Laughter] So it worked out well in the end!

So that just leaves Key Role Four to tell you about. That was the staff training one. Again, the first exemplar I did was on the older adults on the site. We used a particular measurement scale that had been modified for neurological rehabilitation, and it was about delivering training to ward staff and other disciplines on how to use the scale because this was like behavioural model data, so every little bit of aggression, self-harm or a sexualised behaviour is recorded when it happens by whoever's around, and so it was about delivering training to the staff on how to use that. I was training nursing staff and people like occupational therapists as well and anyone who was coming into contact with the patients. The trick with that key role four was the evaluation aspect of it. The first time the assessors kind of gave me a little slap on the wrist, but expected me to improve on it in the second time and basically what I had done was, in terms of evaluation I had done those like "happy sheets", like "did you find the training useful?", "yes or no", and things like that. And then my other part of the evaluation was getting people to rate an actual scenario and see if they had acquired the necessary skills following the training. What they (the assessors) were looking for was a long-term follow-up as well, which I hadn't done. But they allowed me to pass as long as I improved on that in my next exemplar, which was good because they gave me that opportunity. I'm not sure if the assessors are that generous anymore. So, it seems more difficult now in that trainees can't learn from their mistakes in the first exemplar.

So on the first occasion I delivered a training package that I had made slight changes to but which already existed as a written training package. The second time I developed the training package from scratch and I think again it was an expectation that you did that. So, for the second exemplar I decided to deliver training to staff on managing stress related to working with a challenging client group; and that's difficult because you know, it's like finding all the fun ways of teaching people and making it interactive and fun and all of that and then the evaluation procedures involved - again the happy sheets. Then assessing their actual basic knowledge on what had been taught afterwards. Also I gave them the "general health questionnaire" to rate their stress then and then I contacted them all three months later via a mini-survey; this time I asked them to administer the general health questionnaire again and for confidentiality purposes never asked for their scores but asked them to tell me whether their scores had changed since their initial rating when they came in before the training. And then I also just completed a small survey to get some information from them about how they had used the skills taught and things like that, which was what the BPS now wanted. So it was pretty comprehensive.

But one thing I must say is that the Red Book, your guideline book for Stage Two, stipulated that you needed to go to this depth. The book stated quite clearly that these are the things that they were looking for and so I didn't feel it was challenging in terms of finding what they kind of wanted in that respect; I was thinking creatively about how to go about and get that and do it, and looking back now, I think that by following what the BPS wanted, really helped me develop and understand all of the aspects that the key roles cover. In general one wouldn't have thought of half the stuff that I actually covered; for example the amount of thought that needs to go into planning or developing a training session. I've used those skills that I developed through my Chartership, again when I have now put together and implemented training subsequently. So I didn't... I have to say I didn't feel once ... well I did at the time, but afterwards I thought well you know, all that jumping through hoops and feeling like the BPS were being pernickety, actually although I was getting really frustrated and thought this was not the real world then, going through that actually gave me the really good grounding in knowledge that I needed to be a proper and effective forensic psychologist. I don't think I would have learned what I had done and I don't think my work ethic would be the level it is and the work that I do produce would be the level it is if I hadn't gone through that rigorous process. I mean I wouldn't say it wasn't traumatic, it was a stressful experience. There were many times in my Chartership I did want to just give up, that I was so drained and so tired and didn't know where I had all the hours because of working full time and then completing all the exemplar work, it's a huge amount of work and so it was tiring.

I didn't have much opportunity to write my work up during working hours. Not really, no, because again I was new and so it was the first time and I didn't have those opportunities as a lot of the trainees do now. I did use to write my practice diary first thing in the morning. That was one thing I used to do at work. Every day I used to come in and do my practice diary for the day before and on occasions when I didn't that was the biggest mistake, because it can take a while and it's a horrible task. I hated it, especially towards the end. I used to get so frustrated with doing the practice diary and the supervision log because it just... [Sigh] because sometimes you think I can't reflect on this anymore you know. But you just have to do it and that's why just making sure you try and do it every single day is the only way to achieve success. It's never easy... you're sitting there for hours and hours and hours trying to remember what you did and trying to reflect in a multitude of different ways. I have to be honest, in terms of professional development; I didn't find the practice diary to be a useful experience. For me, the professional development was doing the exemplars and reflecting at the time on those specific areas. Sometimes some of the reflection that I put into my practice diary or supervision log I would use for my reflective report later on. So it was helpful in that respect. But to be honest with you, I usually see that task as a pain and not very helpful. However, I must add that being a reflective practitioner is essential as a psychologist; you have to get good at that and it is useful. I do remember the first time; I kind of threw myself on my supervisor's [laughter] chair and said 'I don't know how to reflect. What do they mean?' you know "what do people mean when they say, reflect?" and that was... the first thing was getting around; well what are they actually asking? What is reflection? It's a good place to start! [Laughter]

So the majority of (the Chartership work) was done in my own time and that was very difficult. So from that aspect it was draining and then always the high anxiety of waiting for those exemplars to come back and see what the assessors had to say because I will be honest, a lot of the feedback that I used to get, I used to think well "how was I meant to know that you wanted that?", because there was loads of stuff that used to come back in the feedback, they'd passed me, but you'd get really detailed feedback which you could use on the second exemplar and they didn't even mention that in the guidelines (Red Book), so how am I meant to know that that's what they wanted.

I think training in a hospital environment has given me a greater depth and breadth of experience than working in a prison. I mean colleagues of mine who have have been trainees in prisons and trainees I've come across at various CPD events, those who are doing it in the prison service are going through hell. They've being doing their Chartership for five or six years, sometimes taking even longer and are really frustrated by the process and, I can't speak with any actual knowledge about the prison service, but I understand it is because you get hired to work on a specific program that the most you could really ever cover is a couple of key roles. And so it's a point of changing job in order to then start getting the other experience and when you think about how much you have to get through, the prison environment, although it has the majority of forensic psychologists and trainees, isn't set up to train psychologists for Chartership.

I was submitting my exemplars pretty quickly; in fact as soon as I finished a piece of work. I didn't think about it, I put it together, and submitted it, because my view was the sooner I submit this, the sooner I find out if it's okay or not and the sooner you know, things can progress and that motivated me really and it was awful, it was very anxiety provoking, it was absolutely awful. Every time the post used to come through [laughter] and I used to come home and see the post on the mat, my heart would literally go and when there was a letter, an assessor report, it used to take me five minutes to try and overcome the nausea. Honestly, that's how bad it was. But you can't avoid things because you're scared of it and in a sense I felt, well, rather do it and find out so that you can do what's necessary. Otherwise I'm going to be doing this for ten years and so I think that's what pushed me. I know a lot of my peers have withheld submissions because they think they will fail.

You have to be very proactive in managing your training; whether it's trying to get people to give you the opportunity to do some work experience in the first place, or whether it's getting those exemplars written up and submitted. There was no one there to nag and push me, I just kind of had to do it, and if I wanted to get chartered and be a qualified psychologist, well then that's what I had to do; and I achieved it! Because the whole process was very new to both of my supervisors, neither of them had done this before, they kind of left me to my own devices and very often I was just telling them what they needed to do; if supporting letters or things like that were needed from them, it would be me telling them what needs to go in the letter [laughter] and stuff like that.

I am really enjoying my career now. I love working with adolescents, absolutely adore them. I don't think I'd want to work in any other field with any other client group again. Having worked with older adults at the other end, I used to find that quite a depressing task; it can be easy to think, "what's the point? Things just aren't going to change." Sometimes patients would die just after I had risk assessed them; that is the reality; whereas the adolescents can progress quickly through the service. It's very high pressured because you have to work at a far quicker pace, but you can make the difference at this stage. You do see movement, you do see improvement; you're getting them pretty young; not when they're adults. The adolescent unit takes people between the ages of 13 and 21. Some are moving down through the security system but some will inevitably move up to high security. Remember our service is Independent; and we do seem to get the worst end of the scale in terms of challenging behaviour; a lot of NHS placements won't take these adolescent offenders because they're seen to be unmanageable.

Would I do anything differently if I was starting over again? No, I wouldn't; but I think I can say that because it went pretty well and pretty quickly. But there again, sometimes I say I've been lucky and sometimes I say well no, it wasn't luck; I did work really hard to do it and made the opportunities and nagged loads of people and I'm telling you about all the ones (job applications) that were successful; but if I try thinking back at how many outright rejections I got and funny looks and oh gosh, "don't even answer the phone if she calls" kind of thing, there's a lot of that. But I wouldn't change anything. I'm happy I did my forensic psychology training through this route.

It worked for me to complete the MSc before really starting the training. There is the alternative option of taking the BPS exams (*this route is no longer available)*; I met some people who did Stage One through the BPS exams but that was not for me; it sounds quite an isolating experience. So my advice is to get on to an MSc course as soon as you can because there's an assumption it's easy to cruise onto one and they're getting very competitive now. So, go and get the work experience and get onto an MSc and start that. And then, my advice, as soon as you can, is to find someone who will supervise you. I wouldn't get too het up on trying to find a trainee post. I'd focus on finding a supervisor and let that be the first point of call and then just use the BPS guidebook as a bible and find yourself someone who's been through the route. I am now the co-ordinating supervisor for one of the trainees here, and at least I can support her with my experiences on Chartership. It's really important to keep people motivated. To be honest with you, so many people I have seen have just given up on the training. They've called it quits. I think back on the people on my MSc course;

I'm not even sure... as far as I know hardly any of the twenty students are qualified. Even the trainee who is coming later on for some supervision emailed me last week saying "I've had it, I'm quitting" and I said "no, you're not, [laughter] you're absolutely not, you come and see me and you're not" and I suppose... It is, it's very hard, but "don't give in", is what I'll say. Don't give up; it is worth it in the end. I love being qualified and doing what I do and it was all so worth it. [Laughter]

Sally Lopresti *is a recently chartered forensic psychologist who commenced her training in HM Prison Service but who subsequently completed her training as an associate working in the independent sector.*

I'm ashamed to say that I started my training as far back as 2004. I was employed by HM Prison Service and working in a high security prison at the time. I was one of the first Forensic Psychologists in-training (FPiT) to join the 'new' competency-based route. The new route was very different to previous routes and it took me, my supervisors and colleagues a long while to fully grasp what was required. In retrospect however, I am also able to point the finger firmly at myself for taking such an avoidant approach to anything chartership-related.

The remainder of this piece is a reflection upon my entry into the field of forensic psychology, my experiences as an FPiT, both as an HM Prison Service employee and as an independent practitioner and the benefits, but also the pitfalls, of trying to complete Stage 2 within both contexts. It is important to note my caveat, which is that I left HMPS in May 2008 and I understand that there have since been a number of changes to the way in which psychological services are structured within the service. Similarly, there are many models of independent practice and so my experiences may not directly relate to those of other FPiT who are working independently. I think, however, that the majority of the points I raise remain valid and are broadly relevant.

Career Change

Having left the University of York in 1998 with a BSc (Hons) in Psychology, I returned to my home town and continued to look for training opportunities within the field. A friend offered a room in a shared rental property near London and I took the view that there may be a greater number of training posts in that area than my home town. Whilst continuing to search for jobs, I secured temporary work to pay my rent. Four years, two temping jobs, a permanent contract and two subsequent promotions later, one thing had led to another and I was an account manager employed by the Bank of Scotland within its motor finance division; responsible for a multi-million pound contract. Things had turned out okay, but by 2000-2001 I had become aware that this type of work was offering limited job satisfaction and I felt compelled to engage in work that was within the healthcare, counselling or psychology field. This need was partly fulfilled when I successfully trained as a Samaritan Listener. I was volunteering alongside like-minded people and I felt as though I was actually making a difference to people's wellbeing, despite how clichéd that may sound.

My voluntary work with the Samaritans confirmed to me that I wanted to return to psychology, or a related field, and I started to apply for jobs. One of the jobs I applied for was a psychological assistant post, advertised by HM Prison Service and based at their head office in London. I was invited to interview, which involved a number of different forms of assessment, including psychometrics, exercises using SPSS and a formal interview. Although unsuccessful in gaining the post at head office, I was subsequently contacted by the head of psychology at a high security prison, who explained that my details had been passed to her due to my positive performance during the assessment day. I was invited to interview for a psychological assistant vacancy at the prison and was consequently offered the post.

I did not specifically target forensic psychology; some colleagues had a longstanding ambition to enter forensic work, but I was happy at that stage to enter any psychological field. I haven't looked back since starting my career and continue to find my work fascinating.

My experience within HM Prison Service

When I look back at my career as an FPiT within HM Prison Service, I am enormously appreciative of the breadth of experience I gained. When I say 'breadth', I'm referring to the job roles that I held, the core roles that I fulfilled, the client group that I treated/assessed/supported and the range of professions that I worked alongside. Having joined HMPS in 2002 as a psychological assistant, I was successful in gaining promotion to the grade of FPiT the following year. In the five years that followed I filled the following roles: research psychologist (assessing staff coping styles), drug treatment programme facilitator, drug treatment programme treatment manager, lead risk assessment psychologist, and discrete unit team leader (Segregation Unit, Healthcare and Close Supervision Centre). Throughout this time I was also a wing psychologist on the vulnerable prisoner unit, working predominantly with sexual offenders and prisoners with mood and personality disorders. When I consider my experience within the context of each of the four Stage 2 Core Roles, I had ample opportunity to engage in Core Role 1 work (interventions and assessments), for example. As well as delivering and managing drug and alcohol treatment, I completed Category A and parole reports, which included the use of structured risk assessments such as the HCR-20 (Historical Clinical Risk), the SARN (Structured Assessment of Risk and Need – sexual offenders) and the SARA (Spousal Assault Risk Assessment). Later in my HMPS career, I had the opportunity to engage in treatment work within the Close Supervision Centre.

The input of psychological services was valued by the Governor and the forensic psychology team was involved in a range of initiatives across the prison. For example, I had the opportunity to play an instrumental role in setting up the establishment's new Risk Assessment and Management Unit, which incorporated the parole, sentence planning, OASys (Offender Assessment usually completed by Probation) and psychological risk assessment sections. I took the psychological lead in this process, which involved creating a new way of feeding psychological assessment and treatment work into the sentence management process. I was responsible for overseeing the improvement of OASys assessments, which involved supervising OASys reports, as well as engaging in professional development / support supervision sessions with the OASys assessors.

Other consultancy roles included attendance at sentence planning boards, mental health reviews, suicide /self-harm risk reviews, segregation reviews and officer recruitment interviews. The opportunities to undertake Core Role 3 (consultancy) and Core Role 4 (training) work were plentiful. Core Role 2 was, in my experience, the more difficult of the core roles to undertake within HMPS. This was not because of a lack of access to participants. Rather, it just didn't seem to fit within the day-to-day priorities of the business. For me, it was very much additional work that I did on top of "the day job".

Being an independent practitioner now, I am far more appreciative in retrospect of the level of training that I had access to as an HM Prison Service FPiT. I have since had to self-fund Stage 2, as well as CPD (Continuous Professional Development) events and opportunities. My two-year part-time MSc in Applied Forensic Psychology (2003-2005) was fully funded by HMPS, although there was an assumption that the week's work would fit into the remaining four days when I wasn't attending the University of York. I saw this as the pay-off for having the course funded, but it made for a challenging couple of years. I was also fortunate enough to receive training in motivational interviewing, therapeutic (CBT) skills, the PCL-R (Psychopathy Checklist – Revised), the WAIS-III (Wechsler Adult Intelligence Scale), supervisor skills, the HCR-20 (Historical, Clinical Risk), SVR-20 (Sexual Violence Risk) and SARA (Spousal Assault Risk Assessment), to name but a few. This is nothing to be sniffed at; the courses typically cost £500+ to attend.

In addition to the training I attended, my BPS/DFP membership was funded by HMPS, as were my Stage 2 fees. In the heyday of my HMPS career, I had regular access to my co-ordinating supervisor and was surrounded by a range of other chartered forensic and clinical psychologists with a variety of backgrounds and experience, which they seemed happy to share with me. The training costs are all factored into the pay package. The working hours were long and there was an expectation that I would take on responsibilities that were arguably above my pay grade. When I left my FPiT role in 2008, having been at that grade for five years, my salary was in the region of £18,000 gross per annum. I had been responsible for service delivery, meeting key performance targets, line management of other FPiT and had supervised prison officers who were earning £10-15k more per annum than I was.

So why did I leave HMPS?

The culture and regime changes brought about by the change in management at my workplace led to a significant amount of disillusionment on the part of many of my colleagues, as well as a sense that the profession was becoming increasingly devalued within that particular setting. One by one the remaining chartered psychologists left. The Stage 2 FPiT highlighted to managers that we were unable to practice without a chartered forensic psychologist to supervise our work and so we arranged for an independent forensic psychologist to visit the prison on a monthly basis in order to provide the minimum requirement in terms of supervision. I was consequently offered the opportunity to join the chartered psychologist in independent practice.
Looking back, my experience of being an FPiT in HMPS involved a huge amount of learning and experience; not just in terms of how to be a psychologist, but also regarding how to consult, supervise and work in a truly diverse and multi-disciplinary setting. In my view, I am a far more assertive, confident and competent practitioner than I would have been had I not undertaken most of my training within that prison.

I wouldn't rule out a return to HMPS in the future, but I'm not ready yet. My time in HMPS was a real baptism of fire. I worked extremely long hours, including unpaid overtime and often felt as though the task was pretty thankless. I didn't prioritise chartership because everything else felt so hectic and more time-bound. Days (particularly as a manager within the team) were spent dealing with crises and evenings were spent getting the "bread and butter" work done. I'll always remember my head of psychology coming to say goodnight to me on her way out of the department at 8pm one evening. She remarked, "Are you working late again? Still, it's the key to success" (paraphrased). I'm not sure I can agree with that; I don't think it's sustainable in the long term and if I had my time again I would take a much healthier and robust approach to my work-life balance.

My experience as an independent FPiT

Since leaving HMPS in 2008 I have been self-employed as a sole trader. I am an associate of an independent forensic psychology practice whose director was also my coordinating supervisor when I was in training. The way our business model works is that the company is instructed to undertake assessment and treatment work, and the work is then allocated to its associates. The majority of my work as an FPiT was instructions by solicitors and tended to relate to preparing psychological risk assessment reports for the purpose of parole hearings. However, I have also worked in association with, and under the instruction of, HMPS; undertaking risk/need assessments and cognitive behavioural treatment with offenders. The HMPS work has increased significantly since I gained chartered status due to their preference to contract qualified and registered independent forensic psychologists. I get to dictate to a large extent how much work I want to take on. This has to be done with some degree of planning in order that the company director knows which cases to allocate to me. However, it has meant that I have been able to dedicate chunks of time to focusing upon chartership work and submissions. When I was working for HMPS I really struggled to focus upon chartership because my workload was so high and there were always more immediate deadlines to be attended to. As well as undertaking work in association with writing risk assessments, I have sought out experiences elsewhere. In some cases these have been in order to fulfil the requirements of chartership (for example, undertaking some research at a London prison), but others have been in order to further my own professional development and build upon professional links with other practitioners and institutions (for example, lecturing on an MSc in Forensic Psychology course, and marking GCSE psychology papers for an examination board). Self-employment allows me to be my own boss and, within the confines of my own financial commitments and the need for my practice to be supervised, the world is my oyster, so to speak.

So what are the pitfalls of being an independent FPiT?

Working from home takes great discipline and my personal experience is that I never achieve as much in a day as I plan to, so my financial projections may not always play out. I'm lucky that I have colleagues (associates) with whom I get along extremely well and we make a point of meeting up on a monthly basis for peer supervision, as well as the more frequent emails and telephone conversations that provide some element of human contact. This helps not only to mitigate the loneliness element of home working, but also provides an opportunity to share and challenge ideas; a key part of maintaining good standards of practice.

Not all independent FPiT are necessarily self-employed. However if you are, you need to consider the costs associated with our work. I pay my own BPS and DFP membership; I funded my annual maintenance fee, supervision fees and the costs of submitting exemplars for assessment. I also pay for my office supplies, professional indemnity insurance, my CRB checks, my registration with the Information Commissioner's Office (Data Protection) and any training or conference fees. As a self-employed practitioner I get no paid annual leave, sick leave, maternity pay or pension. Being self-employed means that, when times are good, I can earn significantly more than is possible as an HMPS employee of equivalent grade and experience. However, work can go through fits and starts, which can be an issue when there are regular bills to be paid. Good personal discipline in financial planning can go a long way to mitigating this, and in my own case I'm part of a dual income household where my partner has a more regular income that reduces the financial risk associated with this.

My "bread and butter" work tends to relate to assessments and interventions, providing me with ample experience of Core Role 1. Undertaking work in relation to the other core roles required me, as an independent practitioner, to be proactive in seeking out opportunities. Fortunately, I had completed exemplar work for Core Roles 3 (consultancy) and 4 (training) prior to leaving HMPS. I was able to use professional connections I had made during my time in HMPS to secure access to participants in order to undertake Core Role 2 (research). The potential for a good breadth of work as an independent practitioner is great, but I think you have to work a bit harder at it.

So, what did I do to complete Stage 2 Training?

For the majority of FPiT, Stage 1 of the Qualification in Forensic Psychology is satisfied through completing an accredited MSc degree programme in forensic psychology. Stage 2 involves the submission of work for assessment. Two exemplars must be submitted for each of the four core roles: Assessment / interventions; Research; Consultancy; Training. Alongside this work, daily practice diaries must be kept, including a log of supervision sessions. A competency log must be maintained and quarterly supervision plans written in collaboration with your supervisor. When you come to present core roles for assessment, a reflective account of the work must also be submitted.

As one of the first generation of FPiT to commence the current route to chartership I was very unclear as to what my exemplars should "look like" and what the benchmarks were for passing or failing submissions for assessment. This was compounded by my entry into independent practice in 2008, which meant that I had a much smaller cohort of FPiT colleagues to share experiences with. I am now going to share my exemplars with you and provide examples of work that has been deemed appropriate for submission as exemplars of the four core roles.

Core Role 1: Conducting Psychological Applications and Interventions

Exemplar 1A - Conducting a range of structured risk assessments with prisoners to inform the Parole Board of level of risk of re-offending and outstanding treatment needs.

I submitted three case studies for assessment:

i)   Case 1 was a Category C prisoner who had been convicted of offences relating to possession of child pornography. He also had some history of generalised violence. I was asked by his legal representative to undertake a psychological risk assessment in preparation for his client's upcoming parole hearing. In order to assess levels and nature of risk and need I considered the use of the Risk Matrix 2000 (RM2000), the Risk for Sexual Violence Protocol (RSVP) and the International Personality Disorder Examination (IPDE) Screening Questionnaire. I utilised the most appropriate assessments.

ii)   Case 2 was also a Category C prisoner who had been convicted of the rape of an adult female. I was asked by HMPS to conduct a Structured Assessment of Risk and Need (SARN) following the offender's completion of sex offender treatment and in preparation for his upcoming parole hearing. The individual appeared to experience some barriers to progressing in treatment, which I explored and subsequently made a recommendation for an assessment of executive functioning.

iii)   The third case related to the provision of a psychological risk assessment to contribute to an offender's upcoming parole hearing. The individual was a Category C prisoner serving a mandatory life sentence for the murder of an adult male. The offence involved callous and excessive violence. In assessing risk and need I applied the HCR-20 (Historical, Clinical, Risk Management) tool as well as the International Personality Disorder Examination (IPDE) Screening Questionnaire. In formulating the case I recognised symptoms consistent with Attention Deficit Hyperactivity Disorder, which appear to have impacted upon previous treatment outcome, and so recommended assessment in this area.

Exemplar 1B - Undertaking treatment need analyses and/or individual treatment work with offenders with a view to further reducing their risk of re-offending.

Again, three case studies were submitted:

i)   The first of these cases related to a Category A prisoner who had recently relocated to the prison estate having spent over a decade in secure psychiatric units. His convictions related to acts of violence with a strong sexual element. He also had an extensive history of committing non-contact sexual offences. I received a referral from Sentence Planning Board members to undertake a Structured

Assessment of Risk and Need (SARN) in order to identify outstanding needs and make recommendations for future treatment avenues. This resulted in a referral to the Dangerous and Severe Personality Disorder (DSPD) service.

ii)   The second case related to a Category A prisoner located in a Close Supervision Centre (CSC). He had requested engagement with a psychologist in order to explore his offending behaviour. Having first had to demonstrate the feasibility of this work to more senior managers, I undertook six sessions of cognitive behavioural treatment exploring the function of the individual's acts of violence and violent ideation, with a view to identifying pathways for future treatment and risk management.

iii)   The third case study related to a Category C prisoner who had been precluded from attending the HMPS accredited Healthy Relationships Programme due to certain aspects of his offending. The independent psychology practice that I am associated with was contacted by the lifer manager at the individual's prison and asked to undertake a risk and need assessment followed by a course of treatment to address risk of spousal assault, if deemed appropriate. Based upon the needs identified I subsequently delivered six sessions of cognitive behavioural treatment which were rooted in psychological theory linked to both attachment style and patterns of violence akin to the client's.

Core Role 2: Research

Exemplar 2A - Assessing the predictive qualities of the Offender Assessment System (OASys) in relation to Psychopathy Checklist - Revised (PCL-R) score among adult male prisoners in HM Prison Service's High Security Estate.

PCL-R scores were gathered as part of the data collection stage of a large needs analysis being conducted within HM Prison Service's High Security Estate between January and May 2008. For each of the offenders for whom PCL-R scores were available, full OASys assessments were also collected. Logistic regression was performed to assess the reliability of selected OASys risk items in predicting PCL-R outcome. The discussion section of my research report outlined strengths, limitations and applications of the study and its findings, as well as directing future research.

Exemplar 2B - An explorative study of hopelessness and the effect of ethnic background upon level of suicide risk amongst adult male prisoners.

My aim in conducting this study was to identify whether previously reported differences between ethnic groups in relation to suicidality were upheld once a significant psychological factor – hopelessness – was controlled for. The study drew upon data from a larger scale doctorate study with which I was involved. Data was collected over a three-month period from prisoners within the first days of their arrival within a Category B prison. This allowed researchers to measure psychological variables, including hopelessness and suicide risk, whilst prisoners were experiencing a period of particularly high risk of self-harm or suicidal behaviour. An analysis of co-variance was conducted to compare the significance of two factors known to affect risk of suicide (ethnic group and level of hopelessness). As with Exemplar 2A, the strengths, limitations and applications of the study were outlined in the Discussion section of my research report, alongside directs for future research.

Core Role 3: Communicating Psychological Knowledge and Advice to Other Professionals

Exemplar 3A: Developing the contributions of psychologists to risk assessment and management at HMP X.

In December 2005 I started a new role as the Lead Risk Assessment Psychologist. This coincided with the initiation of processes by which a number of teams, including Psychology, Probation, Sentence Planning, CARATs and Offending Behaviour Programmes would all merge to become the Case Management Function. The new approach meant changes to the way in which psychologists contributed to sentence planning and risk assessment. I was tasked with conceptualising and implementing these changes. The most significant of these included: Designing, implementing and managing the new OASys+ psychological risk assessment service; Developing strategies for psychological input to Risk Assessment and Management Boards (sentence planning); Improving the quality of OASys assessments, through training and supervision of assessors and their supervisors.

Although the organisational changes had the full backing of senior management, there were members of the new function who were strongly opposed to the restructuring and seemed particularly resistant to the influential management roles awarded to senior psychologists as part of the new strategy. Practice diary and supervision log entries demonstrated ways in which I developed new skills and knowledge in order to overcome, over time, these team dynamics so that I could deliver the psychological input that was required.

Exemplar 3B: Providing a psychological contribution to the selection of uniformed staff for HMP X's Discrete Units.

In January 2008 I was temporarily promoted to Manager F and took the position of Research and Short Interventions Team Leader. The team's primary purpose was to offer a psychological input to the establishment's discrete units, including segregation, healthcare and the CSC (Close Supervision Centre). This exemplar focused upon two pieces of work that I carried out in relation to discrete unit staff selection. The first involved working alongside the segregation unit's principal officer in order to develop a staff selection interview. I went on to interview candidates for officer and senior officer positions and subsequently provided candidates with written feedback on their performance. The second project was carried out in collaboration with the CSC's principal officer. In this case, we reviewed the existing staff selection process and updated it in order that it mapped onto the new Competency and Qualities Framework (CQF), which had been recently launched by HM Prison Service. This included developing a new interview schedule, in line with the competencies outlined in the CQF.

Core Role 4: Training Other Professionals in Psychological Skills and Knowledge

Exemplar 4A: Provision of training for new Focus facilitators.

This exemplar detailed my contribution to the professional development of Focus facilitators. Focus is a substance use rehabilitation programme aimed at providing intensive cognitive behavioural group treatment to prisoners with severe histories of drug and/or alcohol use. I was a Focus facilitator between January and August 2004 and was subsequently the programme's treatment manager until October 2005. The exemplar outlined the way in which I was able to apply my knowledge and understanding of the Focus programme to supporting the treatment manager and wider treatment team at a time when professional development needs were high due to the number of new facilitators compared to more experienced ones, but availability of resources to address training needs were relatively low.

Exemplar 4B: Identification of training needs and consequent planning and delivery of training in anticipation of job role changes within Psychological Services at HMP X.

This exemplar demonstrated my competence in recognising a situation where additional training was required, liaising with key personnel in relation to the identification of training needs, design and delivery of training and, finally, evaluating the impact of the training. In September 2007, plans were put in place at the prison in which I worked to significantly change the way in which forensic psychologists in training (FPiT) were able to apply their skills and develop professionally. Rather than being assigned a particular role, FPiT entered a placement system, whereby they would change role every six to 12 months. This was with a view to increasing breadth of experience and learning in order to meet the competency-based approach to chartership as a forensic psychologist. In undertaking the work described within the exemplar, I provided key managers with relevant information regarding the team's skills profile, allowing them to make more informed strategic decisions. I also assisted FPiT and their line managers to anticipate training requirements in order that FPiT could aim to address their skills and knowledge gaps prior to assuming a new role.

My advice to others

I'm glad that I gained my earlier experience within HMPS because it provided me with a range of opportunities in terms of training, access to the client group and multi-disciplinary working. However, I haven't looked back since becoming an independent practitioner. I have a huge appetite for learning and improving and find that I have more time to focus upon my own professional needs now, in order that I can in turn provide a better service to my clients. My words of warning for those considering independent work relate mainly to ensuring that you can secure a co-ordinating supervisor, making sure that you factor in the hidden costs of being a self-employed FPiT, and being prepared for the level of self-directed learning and networking involved.

Seek out employment opportunities within HMPS if you can; especially at the beginning of your training. However, as an HMPS employee, make sure you will have regular access to a co-ordinating supervisor and that you make time for your Stage 2 submissions. I suspect the relatively newly introduced Stage 2 Quarterly Supervision Plans will help in making sure you're moving forward in your training.

Chapter 8: Those who have left and embarked on alternative careers

*"**Kate**" is an Assistant Psychologist working in the NHS. She is about to commence on the clinical doctorate training programme. Kate had previously worked for HM Prison Service as a forensic psychologist in-training where she gained a lot of valuable experience working as a facilitator on sex offender treatment programmes but her restricted role and pressures to complete prison service programme targets impacted negatively on her ability to gain chartership whilst maintaining a healthy work / life balance.*

This is an edited account of an interview that I conducted with Kate. Kate provides a candid account of her journey working with sex offenders and gives advice on managing your own psychological wellbeing.

When I was at university I wanted to become an applied psychologist. I started studying psychology at A-level and at first when we were at school, psychology looked interesting, but I didn't really have much of an idea of what it was all about, then I started to love it. I decided to study psychology at university, against my mother's wishes, then decided I wanted to do applied psychology but didn't... I was put off postgraduate study in clinical psychology actually because it felt very precious and I was sort of given the idea not to consider it... I knew I was probably going to get a 2:1 degree and given the idea that if you didn't get a First you couldn't get into clinical and clinical had been one of the first areas I was interested in, but I was also interested in forensic and there was a career's fair at university and they had a stall, the prison that I eventually worked at had a kind of careers stall about forensic psychology and I went from there, I just read a lot about it, found out about it, went on the prison service website and found out a bit about what the jobs available were and got pretty fixed on that as what I wanted to do. And I contacted the local prison. I contacted HMP X because I had spoken to someone at the careers fair and asked if I could go on work experience and they said in theory yes, but they were very busy and didn't have time to think about it and so I rang them every week for about three months, I kept pestering them and they eventually said "yeah, come in" and that's how I got into forensic psychology.

There was very, very little information about forensic psychology at my university. It seemed to be more academically inclined as opposed to applied. There was no... I don't think we had any lectures on forensic issues. There weren't any tutors that were qualified as forensic psychologists. It just wasn't presented at that time to me as an option. The only way I considered forensic psychology was through going to this career's fair where there happened to be a stall; I didn't know much about it until then.

It's hard to remember why my attention was drawn to the prison service stand at the careers fair. I can't remember when the seed was first sown to examine a career in forensic psychology. I don't remember thinking... I don't remember before that point thinking about forensic psychology, but I think you can't fail to be interested by what makes people tick and particularly in the more-ish way it's like rubber necking isn't it, on the motorway? You want to know about why people commit these horrendous offences and to think about having a role in preventing them was really appealing to me.

I was in the second year of a three-year psychology degree at the time. It was the middle of my second year because I went and did some voluntary work experience at the prison in my summer holidays at the end of my second year. I think it was my perseverance with one member of staff who I made sure knew my name and made sure that I was interested got me the voluntary work. I think that when I eventually got a paid job there, that was way more due to my voluntary work that I'd done when I was, both in the prison, but I also did quite a lot of voluntary and low paid work with children with autism, and as a mentor in secondary schools. I did some one-to-one work with children identified as needing extra support.

As for the duration of my work experience in the prison service, I initially did the holidays, full time for about three weeks in the psychology department which I don't think you can do now unfortunately because of the increased security checks and because of increased data protection and confidentiality policies. So, it was the lady who was at the career's fair that I contacted; I got her name and she was acting head of department and then I just kept ringing her; being persistent and I think that was what got me the placement. I would have got forgotten and put to a bottom of a pile if I hadn't kept ringing probably.

I don't think it was just my prison experience that counted when I tried to obtain paid employment in a prison psychology department. I think I had... I had showed I could work with a range of people. I don't think most people have got forensic experience when they come in to work as assistants, but they generally have experience with people in the broadest sense. For example, I had worked as a one-to-one therapist with a child for about one year. I think he was about eight at the time and on the autistic spectrum. I'd pick him up from school one night a week and go back to his and do some sort of Applied Behavioural Analysis.

I think I learned a lot, but it also let me evidence what my skills were when it came to filling in application forms, because I learned about... well it was my first experience of working, one-to-one with children. So I learned a lot about communication styles and interacting with people with complex needs, what worked best in terms of behaviour change and general behavioural principles. But it also allowed me on my application forms later on to evidence that I could work with people's complex needs I could apply psychological principles, evidence-based principles to my work and all those skills... I don't think the skills that you would use in that job would be any different to the skills that you would use in a forensic psychologist's post. So I think that's the key for people to remember, is you don't have to work with offenders in your work experience, you just have to show you can use the skills that would be needed.

At that time I probably did not have the same insight as I do now that I was applying psychological theory to practice; probably not in the same way I would understand it now, and that wasn't why I applied for the job in the first place, but once I was in the job I could see how what I was learning at University was what I was using in an applied setting. I don't think you need to work in psychology or with offenders to get into psychology from my experience anyway. A lot of the people I've seen have just worked with people who have complex needs in loads of different roles, carers, nurses and all different backgrounds. Obviously the closer you get to the population that you're going to work with, the better. But generally you just need to be able to provide evidence of the skills that you're using.

When I talk about people having complex needs I mean working with people who can present challenging behaviour in loads of different forms. So aggressive behaviour... somebody who worked... somebody, when I was in the prison and we were looking at applicants, somebody had worked in a bar and on the surface you wouldn't think that's that relevant, but they were able to evidence how their interpersonal skills had used them to calm situations and to manage aggressive behaviour and all those kinds of challenging... those skills that you'd need to work with a challenging population like you would have to in the prison. Complex needs I guess can mean a lot of things but it could be finding different ways to communicate with people from different backgrounds, being non-judgemental, all those kind of things.

So I graduated in June 2002 and I got my first paid psychology job in the December. In the meantime I worked for Orange which was after University, as I desperately needed some paid employment; I don't think I even put that job on the application form because I was literally there a couple of months and I thought my other experience would be more relevant. But after that I worked at a further education college as a support worker there with an adult with mainly one-to-one support in the classroom and one-to-one work with an adult student with autism. I applied for the assistant post and the trainee post at the same time, and when I applied for the trainee post it was different to how it is now. You applied to a central recruitment drive... I don't even know who oversaw it, but prison service central body and you went to an assessment centre down in Birmingham and they assessed you as suitable or unsuitable, you were potentially fit and then you had to go back to your establishment where you wanted to work and they would interview you locally, and you had to pass that interview as well which is the route I went through to get a trainee post. Whereas now I think that it's directly with the establishment rather than central recruitment. Anyway, I applied for them both at the same time, so they're all a bit blurred in my recollection. I don't remember an awful lot about the application process except for as I say, I know I emphasised my relevant working experience, rather than that I'd worked in Tesco's or the loads of other little jobs through University in the holidays and stuff so. So making sure I put down the relevant stuff. I remember I had an assessment centre for the assistant post, which consisted of an interview, a role play with someone role-playing an offender and you speaking to them basically.

I liked that assessment because I think if you are good with people, which I think is so central to this work and way under-valued in some places, that allows you to shine in the role-play scenario. Some people go to pieces in interviews and it's nothing to do with the job that... I've seen people physically, you know, shake in interviews and they wouldn't have... they won't be like that in the job. It's the situation that they're in. I felt it gave me an opportunity to be me and show how I could relate to people and I had to do a presentation as well about a problem I had solved. So sort of, I guess that was assessing how I would present to a group, because a lot of the role that I did was group work. There was nobody in the field that I felt that I could turn to at that point to gain advice about preparing for the interview and assessment centre.

I didn't know anybody that already worked in forensic psychology. I knew a few people that were in the prison from going in and doing voluntary work, but not well enough that I felt I could have asked for advice or support because I didn't want to compromise my chances; they were going to be judging me, a lot of them, so I couldn't really speak to them. So I did it pretty much on my own, but I think I'd been at an advantage, I'd definitely been at an advantage being on voluntary work in the prison because a lot of the interview questions were about; "what do you think we do here?" "What's the role of a forensic psychologist?" "What kind of work do you expect you'd be doing?" "What do you know about this group work program?" So a lot of that I'd knew because I'd been there, so that was really helpful.

I was an assistant psychologist for three days! But only because, as I said, I applied exactly the same time for the assistant and the trainee positions and the interviews were within a week or two of each other for the assistant post and for the trainee post and I got the assistant post and started that job and then three days later found out I had also got the trainee post. So I was very, very lucky because it was quite rare and I'm not sure how I managed that. Actually, I think I do know and I think it's been really important in all my interviews, I went to the trainee interview knowing I'd got the assistant post which took off a lot of pressure because it's that foot in the door. I wasn't bothered about getting straight on as a trainee. I wasn't expecting to because I'd heard that it's very difficult and you need to get your foot in the door first and so I had no expectation I would get the job, but revised for it and worked for it and I think when I went to the interview they thought I was confident and actually I was very relaxed and oh okay, well if I do all right, great, if I don't it doesn't matter. I think that probably helped.

In terms of preparation I made sure I knew what the job was that was on offer, not just that it was trainee forensic, but what that specific prison did, what their specific programmes were; I knew a bit from being there, but I also made sure I knew what their main focus of the prison was because different prisons have different roles. To give you an example, I worked at HMP X and it has six wings, soon to be seven, more if you include the segregation wing and the hospital wing. Anyway, six main wings, four of which are for vulnerable prisoners, the majority of whom are sexual offenders. So 90 per cent of your work is with sexual offenders and people have come to work for us and said "I don't want to work with sexual offenders, that's not the kind of... I can't do that work" or "I'd thought I'd be working with this population" and obviously have done no research into the kind of work that they'd be expected to do. I'd advise potential applicants to really consider if they are up for this type of work; treatment programmes for sex offenders. You'd be surprised; I've known of people who join the psychology department and then say they don't want to work with this population. That is fine, as the work is not for everyone but do be honest with yourself.

And I think you need to know yourself. I think that's one of the main things you need to think about; because not all prisons do sex offender work and it's certainly... you can be a forensic psychologist without going in to that. But if you're going to apply to a particular prison and that's the main focus of what they do, then think about whether that's something that you think you can cope. It is difficult to know this when you are young and have just graduated. But I think some people... if you've got personal issues that might be triggered by that work for whatever reason, different reasons, I think you need to really explore with yourself before you apply. Some people might get in the work that they find afterwards that they thought they would cope and they can't and I think that's perfectly reasonable and you've got to look after yourself. But I think you can do a certain amount of reflection before you apply for that kind of work as to whether you think you can be non-judgemental and you think that you have the right approach for it and whether you think it might be damaging for you because it invariably is, but it's to what level. I don't think anybody that I've worked with hasn't been negatively affected in some way by the work, but most people would say that the positives outweigh the negative impact. And I think if it doesn't, I'm not sure you're in the right work because I think the majority of people I've worked with have gone into the job because they want to help people, because they want to prevent those kinds of offences happening because they find them damaging, but they've also got a personal interest in giving people a second chance and rehabilitation and those people are great for the job, but there's been one of two who have seemed quite punishing and others that just seem totally detached from the work and I think if this isn't touching you or affecting you in anyway, then you need to think why because it's awful, some of it's awful, some things you read are awful and I don't think it's a bad thing to be affected by it, but you've got to be able to look after yourself.

I did a lot of groups, sexual offending groups and every group at least once, I would have a horrific dream and it was really random, I never knew when it was coming, but it would happen once in every group, in six months of a group, and it'd be an awful dream and it would always have one of my group members in and wasn't necessarily on the surface the worst of the offenders or the most difficult, but it would just be one of them would be in my dream and then you've got to go into group the next day and not show that and you have the emotional stuff still going on and it's not pleasant, but I got a lot of job satisfaction out of it and I enjoyed it and for me the benefits far outweigh the personal costs.

There is support for group facilitators. I think what the prison service did really well with that work particularly, I'm talking about sexual offender work because that's my main background, but there are lots of other things people do, but with sexual offending work, because we know it has an effect on people, counselling is compulsory. You have to go... it depends on which program you're in, but the six month programs, you've got to go to three sessions within the six months to take the stigma away from it basically, so that people didn't have to feel that they say they couldn't cope, which I thought was a really good thing. So you'll go along and say nothing if you had nothing, but if you needed it, it was there and you could get more. That was the minimum. You could get more if you wanted it. The support is there and I think... I don't want to paint a negative picture of how it affects you because as I say, I think most people have found that they get way more out of it than it costs them. But there are costs and personal costs and you've got to be able to use the support that's there. I didn't tend to use the counselling particularly to deal with stuff. I'd talk to my friends and family. That's how I'm most comfortable. But if you do need it, it's there and it's confidential and only general themes are ever fed back to your employer. So if there are a lot of people saying similar things, that might be fed back, but they would never go and say, "so and so can't cope", unless they thought you were at a serious risk of harm. They have a duty of care to staff in that situation.

Then you've also got your supervisors for support and your co-facilitators and there is a lot of personal support. And people have you know, been working a long time as group facilitators and then sort of said "I don't want to... this is enough, I've had enough now" and that's been my experience. Well actually it's been varied. Sometimes it's been difficult for the facilitator; they've been made to feel that they can't have a break because there are targets to meet. Some other times it's been managed very well and appropriately. But generally it's been good.

So, going right back to the beginning when I first started working as a trainee: I completed lots of IQ assessments, intellectual functioning assessments. I did a lot of psychometric testing for when we do those pre-group and post-group assessments to examine how effective the treatment programme has been. For example on the sex offender work I'd look at measures, attitudes about children and sex, attitudes towards women, relationship style questionnaires, coping style questionnaires, that sort of assessment. So there are the obvious ones like what your attitude towards sex are, but then there's some that's sort of more indirectly related like self-esteem. I was sent on the training programme to be a facilitator very quickly after I started in the prison. That is something that I actually tried to raise as an issue with management because I know people that were sent within their first few days of starting and had no experience of managing groups and it was damaging for them because after they'd failed, because it was pass / fail, and to come back to work having that as your first experience must have been really horrible. The training is thorough and it is hard. People do fail the assessment.

Facilitating groups from early on is very much expected in the prison service because mainly psychology departments main funding comes from programs, and there's always a shortage of facilitators to run the programs because there's quite a high turnover for lots of reasons. There's continually a need to send people away to be trained to facilitate to meet the targets. So there's a tendency to send people perhaps before they should be going, I think. Some people are fine, but some people have found that hard. I enjoyed it. I got my teeth straight into it. But in retrospect, I don't think I was probably ready. I think I probably needed a bit of time to settle in and get to know... I felt enthusiastic and it was all great, but I think probably a bit of time would have been a better way to do things. So yes, psychological assistants where I have worked have been very, very involved in programs as the main part of their job. The program like the enhanced thinking skills, which is about problem solving and managing impulsive behaviour, sexual offender treatment programs and the other program that we ran was a substance misuse program for people with a link between substance misuse and offending, which I didn't work on, but that was the other main area that people could go into and people did have a fair bit of choice of what area they were interested in; that was a quite good thing about where I worked; it was discussed with you and what you would like to do and where possible facilitate it.

As I started doing the programs, I became more involved in doing the evaluation of treatment through writing risk assessment reports. Then I also got involved in the more public protection side of things. So writing parole reports for parole reviews, giving an opinion on risk, a lot of risk assessment, static and dynamic risk assessment work, category 'A', board reviews, life reviews, which was one of the harder things I think about working within a prison compared to working within a health settings. It's... you've got a real dual role, you'd be doing a group with someone one day, working therapeutically and knowing that your therapeutic relationship and trust was the essential building block to change, and then the next day you're writing a report saying this man is high risk and shouldn't be considered for realise at this time and your opinion and you've got to go and disclose this report to this person you've spent six months with, building up a rapport, and it was really hard to do that and damaging to the more therapeutic side of the job and there's ways to manage it and I think if you're a really good therapist, you have an open rapport with someone who can be very honest about where the risks lie and you need to be, but it's still a dual role and it's still who's your client; is it the public, or is it the prisoner, or is it the prison service who you're working for really and it was difficult, because people don't want to tell you things that then two weeks later can stop them getting out of prison and I wouldn't if I was in their shoes. You can see why they wouldn't want to work with you and there's quite a negative connotation surrounding psychology amongst prisoners; they're very suspicious and psychology has a lot of clout and parole boards are very interested in what psychology has to say; psychology probably does not have as much power as prisoners that I worked with used to think you had, but it was very much "you don't want to be saying anything to them" and "keep your mouth shut".

I didn't actually attend any parole board hearings because I was a trainee and we weren't supposed to. That's since changed. But when I was there, it was just you provided a report; you write a report as a trainee, which is signed off by your supervisor so you were rarely required to attend and the board usually didn't call anybody. They would just read the report unless they had specific questions. It was more often lifer reviews because they tended to be more contentious. But trainees have been called to discretionary lifer panels.

So as my role developed I got involved in a lot of the risk management boards, which was sort of the annual review of a plan for the prisoner who would have an MDT meeting to set rehabilitation targets for that year for each person which related to psychology, education, physical health, all different areas. So you would set targets, privileges would accrue if the offender was meeting the set targets. So they get more visits. Psychology was very much part of those boards. I found that the more expertise that I gathered within my role, particularly in sex offending, there was much more of a scope for training of others. Towards the end I did bit of national training. So I then went on to assess other's facilitation skills that wanted to become facilitators so I became the "pass or fail" person of future facilitators.

I'd been facilitating for about five years at this point and I'd done... the core group was the first sexual offender group and it's from medium-high risk to high risk offenders and then when you've become experienced in that there's the extended program which is for high risk offenders and that's a more in-depth program of much more flexibility for the clinician. It uses "schema therapy" work and it's much more responsive. It is still a manual based treatment program but it's more responsive to the individual needs and so you have to evidence a higher level of facilitation skills than for the core program, because you're dealing with more complex needs, higher risk people. So I facilitated on a range of programs and through video... you get video-monitored and assessed on your skill level and then nationally it's coordinated by an offending behaviour program unit, which maintains national standards. They coordinate all the national training, but ask for people from the different bases to support that.

As I said I started as a trainee in the December of 2002 and I enrolled on the MSc degree in September X, part time at York; it was the first year that the programme had been run there and it was really one of the great things about forensic psychology in the prison service as it was paid for and I was given a day off a week to travel and do the MSc. So that took two years. So I finished my MSc in X.

The workload at that time was hard because I didn't get any less work, I was there four days a week but I wasn't allocated any less work to do. So I had to fit my normal job into the four days which was fair enough; I was getting a day off a week to go to York and I was quite happy with that, getting it paid for, but it was hard to fit it in and there was no chance of me getting any other chartership work done, of getting any work for the exemplars done alongside it, unless it fitted into what my role was which the group work side of things continued, so gathering evidence for qualification was easy through that bit. But any other exemplar area there was no chance at that time.

There could have been, there could have been if I had been prepared to take work home every day. I think... I don't think the forensic work's unachievable, but I think you've got to be prepared to take a lot of work home and it depends on how much you value your life balance I think, and I do and what I like about my job... what I loved about my job in the prison was that I couldn't take... certain things I couldn't take home. You can't take confidential information out. You're just not allowed. So therefore you have to leave your job at the end of the day, you go home and you have... and you have to have that. You're working with violent, sexual offenders; you've got to be able to switch off at the end of the day. You can't be doing stuff late at night. So that's one of the things I loved about the job, that you can't take it home, you work in the civil service, you're not expected to do more than forty hours a week and that's nice. But... with your chartership work you can take that, you can be doing your reflective practice and your diary. Putting all your writing... writing all your stuff up and that's what you have to do at the moment if you want to qualify and it wasn't for me.

I finished my MSc degree in X and a year later I was no further forward with my exemplar evidence, because of the pressures of writing reports that were needed for parole reviews. They had to be done, there was no choice. You were required by the courts to do them and you did them. So there was no time for anything else and there wasn't any time... there wasn't any support for having time to do it. So I wasn't any further forward and I'd been there for four years by that point and I decided to take a career break to go travelling, which is something I'd wanted to do since I'd left university but couldn't afford at that time and so I'd been saving and thought that this was the time and again the prison service were great and have a scheme whereby you can take unpaid leave if... it's generally for domestic reasons but it's flexible and if... you have to have things like a good sick record, a good performance record, always got "achieved" on your performance reviews and basically if you're... if you can evidence that you're a valuable member of staff, they will consider giving you unpaid leave for up to five years which is usually for child care and stuff. But, in my case they agreed to give me a year off, they wouldn't guarantee a job, but said "if there's one here it's yours when you get back without going through interviews and stuff". So I was on unpaid leave, went away for a year and when I was away realised that my career wasn't going in the way that I'd hoped it would. I wasn't... I felt like I'd become really good at group work, I'd got a good rapport with the guys that I worked with, I could work with people well in group and on one-to-one, but I still didn't know loads about being a psychologist I didn't feel, at that time. I know about CBT, I didn't know about any other theoretical stances or interventions and I had no scope for individualised work, it was all manual based... you couldn't offer one-to-one, it wasn't feasible because you had 600 prisoners and ten trainee psychologists and two senior psychologists. You physically couldn't offer it because you would be sued for discrimination against people that weren't offered it. It wasn't an option. So you were only doing group work and I enjoyed my group work, but I wanted to be able to... when I qualified I wanted to have somebody sit down in front of me, have someone with different needs be able to sit in front of me and have an idea of different ways to work with them and I felt like if they weren't a sexual offender within a group I'd be a bit stumped and that wasn't what I wanted. I wanted to be a good psychologist and I didn't feel I was becoming one. That was how I personally felt, although I loved my job, I did love my job, I felt stagnant, I felt I'd gone as far as I could with the role I was in and I didn't feel I was getting supervision that I would have liked at that time.

So I looked at other ways I could keep working with offenders, because I did love that, and different routes potentially into psychology if I was to give up forensic psychology or ways I could keep doing forensic but in a different area and I looked at different prisons and they were... I found that all trainees were in similar positions to me. And I then I looked at the NHS and spoke to my current line manager, who's a consultant forensic and clinical psychologist and there was an assistant job going and I applied for it and got it and then spent a week humming and hawing and the employer kept ringing me and saying "we really need you to decide, we really need someone in" and she eventually agreed that I could carry on with my forensic exemplars within the NHS, because you get half a day a week CPD time there which is more than I was getting in prison as a trainee. As an assistant, I was going to get half a day a week to be for my development and I thought that was fantastic, obviously. So she said I would be able to use that time to do my exemplar work, but also my job would include the areas of exemplars that I just couldn't get covered in the prison service. Like research would have been much easier to get hold of and do and there'd be more time to do it. I wouldn't have a big case load, and they said they wouldn't fund it, I'd be funding it myself but obviously in the prison it was funded, but they would support it and she would supervise me and I went there and made my decision to jump and I jumped and then got there and decided I actually didn't want to pursue forensic anymore.

I felt that it was a backwards move in terms of job title. When I found out what the job was though, it was a forwards move to me in developmental terms. It was... I wasn't on a career route; there was no guarantee I was ever going to get on the clinical program. But in terms of my development it was forward, that offered me as a job a way, newer experiences and I was told I would be, depending on my competency, they would have to assess that when I got in the job, but I was confident where I'd come from that I could evidence that I could work with people and had the therapeutic skills, but they hadn't obviously seen them. But providing I could evidence them, I was told I could be able to work one-to-one with patients, with a range of mental health issues, as well as offending history, because it's a medium secure unit; and when I did get there, not only that, I was told to go and design treatment for somebody with schizophrenia who suffered from anxiety and to go and do a literature search and find out how you do that and it terrified me at first because I didn't have a manual. I was like, "just give me the sessions, just tell me how to do it", and she's like "no, if you want to be a psychologist you need to find out what the evidence base is, you need to look how... you need a draw up a treatment plan..." and all of that, I'd never done it before in five years. I'd never... I knew it was based on psychology, obviously I was a trainee psychologist, but you were given the work to deliver. You weren't designing the treatment, the interventions and that was massive for me and my knowledge of psychological theory and treatment has just expanded ridiculously in a year compared to what it was. So yes, it was a backward step in some ways. I'd stepped off one career route in some ways, but personally it was a massive development opportunity that I didn't feel I could turn down.

As I said when I initially went there, I thought I would continue my forensic psychology training and I sat down with my manager and they'd had a trainee forensic psychologist in post at the time. She has actually since left, she has done the same as me, but had been an NHS employed trainee forensic psychologist who'd had exactly the same difficulties as I'd had because she was trained by that organisation in that role and therefore had a case load and again she couldn't fit it into her role, whereas on the clinical psychology program, you're a trainee and you go through different posts and your focus is on that you're a trainee, not... you don't have a case load, apart from... as part of your development. So, they had a trainee there and my manager sat with me and explained the problems that were also there and that, they were sort of universal and would fully support me if I wanted to continue. But once I got there I saw that actually I can still do this job, I can still work with forensic clients as a clinical psychologist, but also if I get bored of that, if I want to branch out, if I want to work in different settings, as a clinical psychologist I can do that and the training route is also way more straight forward, hard to get on, but ultimately time bound and better structured and I just felt if I was going to continue my forensic psychologist training I was still going to have to give up my evenings and weekends, it was still going to take an unspecified amount of time and... I actually only had a limited amount of time left as I was due to finish this May, xxxx. I could have got an extension for a year but there were still no guarantees that I'd get chartered after that. I'm over the moon that I've got a place on the clinical doctorate course, but I've loved my job and it was quite exciting because they only do one-year contracts in the NHS, that was the only scary thing, that most assistant posts are for one year. My boss offered to extend my contract, however she said it wouldn't be in my best interests to stay because if I didn't get on it would be due to not having a breadth of experience. But that was quite exciting to not to know where I was going to go and what work I might get into.

I think I probably will pursue forensic clinical psychology, but I'm open minded about it because I loved... for instance I loved the work I did with autistic students. I really, really enjoyed that in the past and I'll try and get on a placement in my clinical course where I go and do that. I might be able to combine my interest in those two and specialise, very much specialise in that area or I might do something else that I've never done before and love it. So I'm open-minded but I love working in the forensic unit I currently work in. I find it incredibly rewarding; it's a true MDT. I think what I found in the last job a little bit was the MDT was still finding its feet a bit and everyone had their own agenda a little bit. Whereas I found in this job, everyone is generally interested in each other's opinions and there's a real emphasis on the multi-disciplinary approach... There's a meeting every single week about every patient and there's a real working together, on what is going to be good for that person and...

So, now I am going to share my tips about entering applied psychology careers. Well, I think people probably already know that a degree isn't enough. You need to be doing other stuff in your three years at University, getting involved in work experience, not necessarily paid employment. It was the experience that was counted. So you don't have to be employed but getting involved in work... just showing you can work with people that have, as I said, complex needs whatever they may be, whether it's a learning difficulty or a behavioural difficulty or just anything that shows you've got an interest in people and working with people, and do that early because not only does... you know, if you've done it for a week it's not enough... we used to literally score work experience on points and used to calculate how long has this person worked for? Once a week for four weeks, is not many hours, you're not going to get much credit for that. So start early and be consistent, show what you can do if you can. A good degree helps, but it's not the be all and end all. As I said, I got put off clinical but managed to get on with a 2:1 and it never got in my way with forensic having a 2:1.

The profession doesn't need people who are in it because they want to punish people. You need to have warmth towards people and be able to get on with people in your personal life and think about if you can do that honestly and openly, reflect upon yourself, and be reflective in your interview. You don't... I don't think people... people don't need to be saying that they know everything and actually arrogance and sort of coming across as if you know it all is not going to do you any favours. People aren't expecting you to be perfect, but I think that reflection comes in, know what you need to do develop and be open about that, but also know what your strengths are and let people know what those are. Don't be shy to say 'this is what I'm really good at, but actually I don't know this area and that's something I'd like to work on'. You need those skills and if you can evidence them in your form and in your interview, probably more in your interview, it's going to put you in good stead.

Now for those of you receiving rejecting letters I'd offer the following advice. Well firstly, I think we've all been there. I certainly was at various points. But if you're really interested in it and you really want to do it, don't give up, but you might need different experience. So you might need more experience, take your feedback, always get your feedback because it might be something really fundamental that you're doing wrong but it's easily changed. It might be brushing up on policies or equality and diversity issues, or you know, something quite doable. So I'd always get your feedback, always, and do it differently that next time and don't be put off. It is competitive isn't it and I think the last time we recruited we had nearly two hundred applicants for four jobs assistant jobs.

Ermm, so getting a rejection letter isn't any reflection that you're not going to be good at the job. It might just be that you need some more experience, but if you're waiting to get into that role and you're keen, I would say get a job that shows again you're working with people. Don't be working on your own in a library. Make sure you find a job if you can, that you can then put on your form to enhance it. So, as I said, I worked in a college with people with learning support needs. If you can volunteer somewhere that potentially might have jobs afterwards, wherever it is, you're getting your foot in the door early. Get yourself known and be a pest. Be a pest in the right way. I mean... you don't want to be annoying people, but if you show you're eager and you show you're willing and you show you work hard it'll pay off. But you've got to put that investment in and if you give up after your first rejection you probably weren't that keen in the first place, I think. So, persevere.

So would I have done things differently if I was starting over again? I think in retrospect I would have just gone straight for clinical psychology when I left university because you can work with forensic clients in loads of different settings, as outpatients, as inpatients, there's lots of different ways to do that job. I currently work with probation officers and social workers as an assistant in the NHS. There's lots of different ways. But I would have gone into clinical rather than forensic because I think the training route is more established. You're a trainee and you're there to train and you're valued as a trainee whereas there are a lot of problems with the training route in forensic psychology and it's difficult and it's demoralising at times. But, I loved my job, so... and I don't think I would have got on the clinical course if I hadn't had the MSc that it provided me with, the experience it provided me with. So no, I don't think I would recommend, if I'm being honest, I wouldn't recommend the forensic training route to somebody who wanted to be a forensic psychologist. But I got all I could from it. But yes, probably if I was 21 again and making those decisions, I would try and be getting into the clinical forensic setting.
In hindsight, I don't think I knew enough about applied careers in psychology when I graduated. I think by chance I've stumbled upon a forensic psychology stall and found it really interesting. I don't think I gave an awful lot of thought into all the different areas I could go into. I don't think there's any rush. It seems like there is because you've come out of university and you want to become qualified and get paid and there isn't a rush. Just find something, just test the waters, try a few different assistant jobs and they're not badly paid... they're not great compared to your accountant mates that have just qualified, but they're enough to live on and find what you enjoy and then go for it and don't give up!

"Jackie" has previously held posts in a secure hospital environment as an assistant psychologist and as a forensic psychologist in-training. She provides an insight here into her reasoning for leaving the field of forensic psychology and I think that this account should give potential psychologists as well as supervisors some cause for concern and plenty to think about when considering the professional relationship between a trainee and their supervisor. One thing that is clear from this account is that Jackie clearly demonstrates the skill that she practised of being a reflective practitioner and I sincerely thank her for sharing what must have been a very difficult account to write so that we can all hopefully learn from it.

There seemed to be two types of people when I was at school; those that knew what they wanted to do with their life, and those that didn't. A lot of people that I know thought that I was the former and therefore I had always wanted to be a psychologist. But this wasn't the case. I actually wanted to be a doctor; I didn't do Psychology at A Level, in fact I did Biology and Chemistry to help me get closer to my dream of becoming a doctor/researcher and finding the cure for autism (optimistic I know!). Now don't get me wrong, I always had an interest in psychology, a very strong one but I didn't even think of this as a career option until completing my A Levels. I decided to read a book (just because) and I had two choices. One was a book on family medicine and the other a book on forensic psychology; which one did I choose? The forensic psychology one of course (although I cannot remember which one it actually was, there were and still are so many after all!). And it was then it dawned on me...if I find psychology so interesting, do I want to spend the next five to seven years of my life studying boring books on family drugs? After all, it seemed so long. My answer was no and my mind was made up. I researched psychology degrees across a number of universities, and scoured the British Psychological Society website. I honestly couldn't tell you much about my application for UCAS, but I do remember thinking how important it was to get across my passion and drive to study psychology. However, saying that, my work experience and employment at the time helped a lot when gaining a place. While I was completing my A levels, I volunteered at a youth club as a play worker caring for children and young adults with learning disabilities and behavioural problems; a position that I loved and it resulted in me gaining paid employment during the summer months on return from university. Although not actually realising it at the time, this experience allowed me to deal with difficult situations, improve my efficiency in decision-making and helped me to improve my communication skills across different audiences, such as children and their families, as well as work colleagues.

I decided to attend the University of Kent at Canterbury and completed my three-year honours degree (which was BPS accredited - please do not forget about this when applying!). Following this, I applied to complete an MSc in Forensic Psychology; luckily I was accepted as I did not apply anywhere else. By this time, Canterbury had become my home and my friends had become my second family, I honestly couldn't imagine studying anywhere else. While completing my MSc, I realised that my forensic experience was a bit thin on the ground. I had tried writing to a number of psychologists whose details were listed on the BPS website to gain some knowledge and insight into the profession and maybe, just maybe, strike it lucky and get some work experience. But as I was only a student and the fact that the profession is bound by the rules of confidentiality, I received the same reply: "thanks for your interest but no thanks". Luckily I found out about a volunteer scheme at the local HM prison service where they were looking for individuals to help develop offenders' skills and CVs in preparation for their release. Perfect! I also worked as a research assistant for one of my lecturers at the university and thought this would be ideal since research, statistics and methodology is an important factor of psychology (a fact that I was unpleasantly surprised about when starting my course all those years ago). When trying to gain work experience of any kind, whether it is for psychology or not, it isn't about where you get it, but what you gain from it. Transferable skills such as decision-making, communication and problem solving all help to mould a good psychologist; it doesn't matter where you have developed these skills.

Of course being a student of psychology meant that I was a member of the BPS, and therefore received regular magazines detailing different adverts for jobs across the country. Coming from a quiet country area, I was honestly worried about the likelihood of actually getting a psychology-related job when I returned home. Will I be able to get an assistant post? Will I have to move? Will I end up working in a completely different job altogether because psychology is so competitive? I was one of the lucky ones; a friend of mine saw a job for an Assistant Psychologist that was only an hour away from me (easily commutable) and so I applied...and then got an interview...and then got the job! I honestly couldn't believe it! After all my worrying and fretting, I got the first job I applied for. Not all of my friends were that successful. Out of seven of us I was the only one who got an assistant post in the first year after completing my MSc. And I am not saying that I got a job before everyone else because I was better...absolutely not! I just happened to be in the right place at the right time and managed to keep myself from falling completely to pieces during the interview! Psychology is tough and competitive and you will be going for jobs against people who have lots of experience and even a PhD! So you need to be prepared for rejection and constructive criticism.

After waiting what seemed a lifetime for my CRB check to come though, I started my assistant post in a secure hospital environment with offenders. Unknown to me at the time, there were two assistant positions that were advertised and so I started with another girl at the same time. We got on very well and having someone else new to the experience, environment and the job was really helpful for both of us, and we are still good friends now. I absolutely loved being an assistant psychologist, but don't get me wrong...it involved a lot of learning, knowing how to manage my time effectively (which I don't think I have managed to achieve completely, even to this day!) and knowing when to ask for help. This is always something I have found hard to do...mainly because I think that I "should" know it, and therefore I am reluctant to look incompetent or 'stupid' in front of my supervisor or colleagues. Silly I know, but we can call that one of my flaws! Although it was difficult, I got to experience so much in this job role, such as working with a wide range of offenders, both on an individual and group basis. However, the importance of a work-life balance was emphasised by my supervisor - you leave at 5pm and you leave your work at the door. Of course, I was keen to impress and so read up on broad subjects like cognitive behavioural therapy and various diagnoses to "top up" my knowledge...I was like one human sized sponge!

Before I knew it, I had been in this post for almost a year! My partner in crime (the girl I started work with) applied for Clinical Psychology and was successful, which then made me think of my next step...a Trainee Forensic Psychologist post so I could, at last, start my Stage 2 training and be on my way to be a qualified Forensic Psychologist! I was so eager to start, to develop my knowledge and to show people what I was made of...so I started looking for trainee posts both within the area and beyond. During my time in this post, there was already a Trainee Forensic Psychologist working within my department who provided me with a fountain of knowledge, as well as honest and helpful advice. He was always available whenever I had a question or a problem, either relating to work or my future, regardless of how busy he was and for that, I am truly thankful and always will be. Due to his hard work and determination, he soon passed all his exemplars and therefore a trainee forensic psychologist post became available. It seemed only natural to apply; after all, I knew the environment, policies and protocols and I was comfortable in my work. And so I did. And I was the only person to apply and therefore the only person who could take the job. I honestly could not believe my luck and was shocked that no one else had applied. However, in hindsight, this was a problem; feedback from my interview was that it was good but needed improvement, suggesting that I was not quite ready for this position. This was mistake number one.

The second mistake I made was delving straight in. A lot of supervisors will advise that even though an individual may have a trainee post, it is best to take six months to a year becoming familiar with your job role, your environment etc. I thought that as I had already been in this particular work place for a year already, I did not need this time. But I was not prepared for the change in role, how I should view myself and how fellow work colleagues viewed me...it simply was not easy to slip into my new trainee role. Therefore, I would advise anyone to take their time, get a feel for the role and the place, what you expect from others and what your supervisor / workplace expects of you.

So, I started my new job and sent off the paperwork to officially become a trainee with the BPS. Luckily for me, my head of department had organised a supervisor for me and so I was able to start pretty much straight away! Out of all the core roles that I could have chosen, I chose "Assessment and Treatment of Offenders", as I thought it would be the most difficult (I figured get the hardest one out of the way, right?) and yet most interesting of the core roles. Previous to this, I had been an Assistant Psychologist...I had helped to deliver rehabilitation programs, but I had never managed one, or devised a treatment program, or assessed suitability of assessments, and ways of evaluating the aims of the treatment. All of this had previously been decided for me...the work was set and I completed it. Therefore, this was probably the worst core role for me to start with...I had nowhere near enough experience to be able to complete this core role effectively. We can call this mistake number three. Now, I am not blaming other people for my mistakes or for my misplaced eagerness to succeed and do well, but no one else took me aside to shake me and ask me 'what the hell do you think you are doing?' So as the Beautiful South song goes, I "carried on regardless".

Whilst completing this core role, I came across a number of different problems. For one, the environment that I worked in (i.e. mental health, learning disabilities, personality disorders and other complex issues) meant that all patients were complicated and the theory never matched the practice (cognitive behavioural therapy for depression and anxiety never went the way the book says it should!). And so, the patients that I was assigned to work with individually for this core role had a number of resounding issues that I was not experienced enough or knowledgeable enough to contend with which delayed completion of my work drastically. Of course, I had supervision to help provide me with support, but my externally based forensic psychologist supervisor was just that; she was there solely to help me pass as a forensic psychologist and did not know the patients who I was working with. Supervisors from clinical and counselling psychology backgrounds in my work place felt that I should be receiving support and assistance from my forensic supervisor. This of course, caused confusion and breakdown in communication between supervisors and me. I was using psychological approaches that I had never used before and yet was unable to receive consistent guidance and support from my supervisors. When I tried to confront this problem and suggested ways of working to help my confusion, my desperation to gain support was taken in the wrong way, rather it was taken that I was trying to tell other people what to do. And so the problem continued.

Earlier on I spoke about finding it hard to ask for help when I needed it because I was always worried that whatever I would be asking about was something that I should have known all along...I don't know if you remember as I have been rambling on for some time now, but this flaw of mine also came into play here. I was confused as to what I was doing with the patients, but didn't know how to ask for help and was worried about what would happen if I did. So many issues and difficulties came up with the patients (and I am most definitely not blaming them as all of those issues were very important), and difficulties arose between different supervisors, and I found myself slightly rocking in the corner not really knowing what to do! Okay, so I wasn't rocking per se, but you get the drift. This feeling of not being in control or not knowing what was the best step had a knock on effect on my confidence. "What on earth was I thinking?", "I cannot do this", "Why did I ever think that I could do this?" Did this help with my ability to sit down and concentrate on work that I did not understand, on approaches and theories that I had never worked with before and was trying to teach myself? Absolutely not; which of course delayed my work even further.

Just because I was struggling with the work and completing it didn't mean that I just stopped all together. Earlier on, I said about the importance of a work / life balance. Personally, this went out of the window for me. I would flit between not being able to concentrate and stressing myself out about the work that I was *not* doing to working all hours under the sun because I felt bad about not being able to complete the work in the first place. And this was the vicious circle I ended up in for the two years that I was training in this post. And although other work colleagues in the department would talk about the importance of maintaining a healthy work / life balance, they would do the opposite, which also put additional pressure on me to stay late or to come in early. I had days where I thought, "this isn't so bad" and days where I used to physically dread going into work. And due to the nature of the training route, trainees are expected to complete a lot of the work in their own time, as well as completing supervision logs and practice diaries on a daily basis to show reflective learning. Additional pressure and additional work to complete. It can be exhausting doing the same training session or group session every week and trying to think of different things I have learnt and reflecting on these. Another mistake I made was getting behind on these....worst mistake you could ever make so please do not do it!

It was then that my circumstances changed. My forensic supervisor was unable to fulfill this role anymore and so another forensic supervisor was assigned to me. At the time, I did not think that this would be an issue but I came to realise that a different supervisor equals different expectations and a different approach. My new supervisor encouraged me to look at my training in a different way and to identify other projects that I could start working on...you know, being proactive and making the most of any opportunities for research or training that may come my way, rather than being reactive. Personally, I found this approach easier and it almost felt like I was looking at my training from a different perspective. However, I still had two exemplars that were not finished and so this added more things for me to think about and more tasks to complete. This supervisor was also "tougher" on me than my previous supervisor...something which I needed but also came to me as a shock! If I were late even by a few minutes, my new supervisor would pick me up on it. At the time, I felt like I was being told off but in hindsight, my supervisor was teaching me to be professional in all aspects of my job.

My new supervisor looked at all the work that I had done so far (please bear in mind none of which had been sent off to be assessed) and hit me with the bombshell... did not think the work was suitable to pass! After all this time struggling and feeling stressed about it, someone was saying now, not two years ago, but now, that it would never pass. I felt gutted to say the least, and yet the feedback I was given made perfect sense. The cases were not "forensic enough" and were more clinical, I did not have the appropriate experience, the cases were too complicated and I had not been given the opportunities to gain basic training that would have helped with the foundation of my understanding and learning to complete this exemplar. In a way, it was a relief to have someone else say these things, rather than think it was just me not being "clever enough" or "quick enough" to not complete the work, but at the same time I was annoyed that this was not done before. And it is not necessarily anybody else's fault, just unfortunately something that was missed.

I then had to go away to think about what I wanted to do...accept that this work will not pass based on one person's opinion (but a person who appeared to know exactly what they were talking about) or go with my old expression "carry on regardless" and see if a miracle happened! Needless to say, after a lot of thought and deliberation, I decided to let it go and to start again.

Although I felt relieved about starting again, I could not help but have in my mind one single issue...doubt. Doubt in myself, doubt in my work, doubt in my knowledge and doubt in my abilities. I had already tried so hard and look where that had got me?! It was very hard to overcome and it was not just me who noticed it. I was called in to meet with my head of department and although I ended up crying by the end of the meeting, I was very glad for her honesty. Everything that she said to me was what I had thought or noticed myself...when I started I loved my job, now I tolerated it. When I started I felt confident in my own ability, now I doubted every answer I gave in either group or individual sessions. When I started my job, I had skills that would only help me in becoming a psychologist, now I felt that those skills had gone. And most importantly when I started my job I wanted to be a Forensic Psychologist, now I was not so sure. My head of department felt that all these things should not be ignored and that I really needed to think about what direction I wanted to take.

And so I did. I took three long agonising months to make my decision and as soon as I did, I felt liberated and the relief was amazing. I decided that I did not want to be a Forensic Psychologist anymore; and not just a forensic one, but also any type of psychologist. I spoke to my forensic supervisor about my decision and this person was concerned that they may have been "too harsh" on me, but that was not the case at all. This supervisor was honest and respected me and the time that I had put in and for that I am very grateful, because without this supervisor, I fear that I will still be struggling training for a job that I was not sure I wanted to be in the first place.

Some people may read this and wonder what on earth I was thinking, that I threw away countless years of university, experience and training over a 'bump in the road'. But I do not see it like that. All that work and years spent at university will never be taken away from me. When applying for future jobs or degrees or courses, I will always have my two degrees, which says a lot about my determination and my want for knowledge. The experiences I have had whilst an assistant psychologist and a trainee psychologist are my experiences, and I can choose to learn from them. The countless times I woke up early to get into work, to then work late and to do it all over again the next day has highlighted the importance of the saying "work to live, not live to work". My whole life was put on hold for my career and now I realise that work is not the "be all and end all" and I am now the happiest I have ever been. If you spend most of your time dreading or hating your job, then you need to listen and do something about it. A person whom I respected very much during my time as an assistant and trainee psychologist once said to me "admitting that something is not right and that you need to change it takes a lot more courage than continuing to stick with something that does not make you happy." And I believe she was right.

And so I will leave you with these last few words. Establishing yourself in a career can be an amazing achievement, and forensic psychology is interesting, always changing and constantly challenging. It takes determination, motivation, self-learning and the ability to know when you are wrong or need help. If you can see yourself having a career like this and being aware of ever changing theories, approaches and research, then this career choice is definitely the one for you. But you must also be aware that is not easy, it's time consuming, it can be frustrating and you will hate your job at some point! If you keep this in mind, remain focused and hopefully learn from the mistakes that other people have made, (i.e. me!) then you most certainly will do well and go far in the world of forensic psychology and I look forward to hearing about or reading your research in years to come. Take care and follow your heart.

The next chapter offers you an insight into the profession from the perspective of two academics. Firstly, Dr Lynsey Gozna reflects on the process of applying for the MSc in Forensic Psychology. Then "*John*" provides us with some insight into the similarities and differences between clinical psychology and forensic psychology.

Chapter 9: The academic perspective

Dr Lynsey Gozna *is a Senior Lecturer in Forensic Psychology at the University of Lincoln where she is programme leader for the BSc (Hons) Psychology with Forensic Psychology course and teaches and supervises undergraduate and postgraduate students.*

In the first section of this chapter Lynsey explores the route to considering and applying for postgraduate training in forensic psychology and she presents you with tips and issues to consider and ultimately assist you in the process.

Having worked for the past 10 years recruiting and teaching students forensic psychology at undergraduate and postgraduate levels (previously at the University of Surrey and now at the University of Lincoln), I think it is crucial to outline to prospective students and other interested parties the reality of studying in this field, some of the challenges you might face, but more importantly how to try and overcome these. We will discuss the motivation for pursuing a career in this area, gaining experience in forensic psychology, thinking about the right postgraduate course, the application and interview processes involved and future career options. I will also present my own experience of working in this field and some of the challenges faced.

Embarking on postgraduate study in forensic psychology

The field of forensic psychology continues to grow and is an applied field within psychology. The vocational nature of this field, much like Clinical, Occupational and Educational, means that the interest from students is greater because they see a clear career path and have focused ideas about potential employment at the end of study and practice. Undertaking postgraduate study in the area of forensic psychology is the first academic step following an undergraduate degree toward completing Stage 1 toward becoming a Chartered Forensic Psychologist with the British Psychological Society and gaining Registration as a Forensic Psychologist with the Health Professions Council.

It is helpful to reflect on your personal reasons for pursuing work in the field of forensic psychology. It has been said many times to me by colleagues, particularly those working in clinical and forensic psychology, that we are drawn to those areas that affect us personally. This can involve mental health issues (e.g., eating disorders; personality disorders; mood disorders), personal victimisation (e.g. child or adult sexual offences, stalking, domestic violence) or broader need to understand certain behaviours (e.g. paraphilias, serial homicide, and sexual sadism). My experience of supervising and working with students during my own time in academia has led to discussions of all of these areas and can have a negative impact whether relating to academic taught content, research topic areas or practice work with client groups. Although such issues do not always impact on the work of individuals, there are occasions when it is helpful for academics and supervisors to understand relevant information and identify areas where there might be vulnerability. My reasons for mentioning this issue at this stage is to outline the importance of understanding why you might want to work with a particular client group or in an applied forensic setting.

Gaining experience and a realistic knowledge

One of the most important aspects of having aspirations to work as a forensic psychologist is that you have a realistic understanding of the work involved and relevant experience. This is why Stage 1 covers the academic elements and Stage 2 focuses on applied practical experience under the supervision of a qualified forensic / clinical psychologist. Although the knowledge from an academic standpoint is vital so that you have a clear understanding of the field, there really is no substitute for good experience in this field, particularly with the range of offenders, personalities and types of work involved. This not only gives you an insight into the field but will also aid your own personal development, which is essential. Experience assists the academic study and the academic study assists experience – it really is a dependent link. Therefore it really is beneficial to have spent time in the period leading up to any application for postgraduate study to gain experience, if possible throughout your undergraduate studies. What actually constitutes relevant experience will depend on where you are located and the options available to you, however it is important to think outside the box and to consider transferable skills.

Ultimately the field of forensic psychology is about working with people from all walks of life at different stages within the criminal justice system who have some link to crime. This means you might find yourself volunteering as an appropriate adult at police stations, getting involved in victim support or rape crisis, or supporting witnesses giving evidence in court. You could be working in bail or probation hostels, with homelessness organisations, charities in the area of suicide intervention, mental health, and alcohol and drug awareness and outreach. You could be assisting ex-offenders in education and employment or mentoring young people through youth offending programmes. You could be involved in restorative justice, adoption services or parenting classes. Hence you do not need to work with an entirely forensic client group to gain relevant experience – but you do need to know how your experience is transferable. There are some excellent websites with detailed information on volunteering in the criminal justice system or with health and social care settings. The main thing is to be enthusiastic, proactive and committed to any experience you decide to do. Some of these opportunities may involve security clearances, particularly if you are working with children and other vulnerable groups, so take this into account and expect these processes to take between three and six months.

Choosing a course

Across the UK the entry requirements for consideration for an MSc Forensic Psychology degree is a 2:1 or higher in a BPS recognised degree (obtaining Graduate Basis for Certification) or, if you are an overseas student or have completed a different degree (e.g., Law, Biology, English) to complete a Psychology conversion degree prior to applying for postgraduate study. In order to complete Stage 1, all students must now complete an accredited MSc Forensic Psychology degree. Accreditation means that the postgraduate degree has met the knowledge and content requirements of the British Psychological Society and this is a rigorous process that courses have to undertake every five years where the content of courses and associated staff are assessed by an independent panel.

There are a significant number of options available around the UK, full and part time, although due to the range of similar sounding courses available, it is vital to ascertain whether the course you are interested in applying for has accreditation. My advice to students who are interested in the field in general but are still unsure about whether or not to pursue Stage 2 toward chartership and full membership of the Division of Forensic Psychology, BPS, is to undertake an accredited MSc and to leave your options open. This allows you to pursue related forensic careers (e.g., join the police) or to seek employment as a Trainee Forensic Psychologist or similar to work toward chartership.

Although there is a range of accredited courses available, it is important to look at the following when considering where you might want to study. For some students, staying on after undergraduate and remaining at the same university is an option, sometimes due to work commitments or the support of family in the vicinity. For others, moving to an entirely different city is the better option. The location of where you study can be as important as the University itself, the content of the course, or the academics teaching you. There tend to be different emphases across courses and it is for this reason that you should consider what you are the more interested in. For example, some courses will have a significant slant on the investigation of crime from a policing and general law enforcement perspective, whereas others will focus more on post-conviction settings, such as prisons or hospitals (forensic mental health). Other courses might consider witnesses and victims in general whereas other courses focus specifically on children. You need to look at the content of the courses you are interested in and make sure that this is going to be of interest to you – particularly if you have a particular career path in mind.

Remember that a proportion of the taught aspect of the course will be statistics. Usually courses comprise six forensic psychology modules, two research methods / statistics modules and an independent thesis / dissertation. If you are particularly weak at statistics, or feel that applying for full time student status on a course would be too difficult, consider going for a part time option. This allows more time to complete assignments and less pressure in deadlines. The one-year full time MSc is challenging – assignments are longer and more varied and complex than at undergraduate level and often times, deadlines are closer together. However with the part time option comes the potential for employment and this can also reduce the time you have to focus and study. If you are not sure which study option is more suited to you, speak to the admissions person at the University you are applying to and gain their advice.

The thesis / dissertation is an independent piece of research that students conduct as part of the MSc and are supervised by one member of staff at the University. Depending on the links that the University have or your own personal links, it might be that you conduct your research in collaboration with an external organisation and that they provide a point of contact / supervisor for you to liaise with "in-house". The thesis accounts for a third of the course credits on the MSc course and is therefore a significant piece of work. You need to be prepared to engage in this research to a higher standard than would be expected at undergraduate and to conduct a substantial study which could ultimately be published in a peer reviewed journal. This involves initiative, independent working, confidence in research methods and the willingness to understand the particular research area in-depth.

The application process

There are variations in the time frame that universities will consider applications from prospective students and therefore the sooner you have made the decision to apply for the next intake, the sooner you should put together your application. The process usually commences between Oct/Nov to May/June of the year of intake. However check the timescales for the course you are interested in to make sure that you meet their individual deadlines.

Aside from the generic information required in an application for the MSc Forensic Psychology, students are required to write a personal statement or supporting statement. In my experience these come in various forms and having read hundreds of these, I have some suggestions as to what makes for a good statement:

1. Plan what you are going to say – this might seem obvious but make sure that all the content of your statement is relevant to the course you are applying for and focused on the particular institution. If you are applying for more than one course, make sure you tailor your statement accordingly.
2. Think about the reality of forensic psychology and make sure you present your experience and knowledge in a mature and appropriate way.
3. The motivation you have for choosing this career, particular course or university are important and therefore include this in your writing.
4. Write with the course in mind – remember that this is a professional training course and you should emphasise your practice experience and also your academic pedigree. Include information about your undergraduate independent dissertation and other relevant academic information.
5. Think about what makes you stand out as an applicant and emphasise what it is that makes **you** appropriate for consideration onto the particular course.

The interview / assessment

Depending on where you apply to, you might receive a straightforward acceptance onto the course, invitation to interview or to an assessment day. If you are invited to a university for an interview / assessment, make sure you prepare in advance for this. Think about the course and make sure that you have a good understanding of the content and staff involved in the teaching. Interviews tend to cover areas such as your motivation to apply for postgraduate study, your academic background including prior research, and your practical experience. If you are asked to take part in an assessment day, this can variously include a research methods task, group exercise, a writing task, presentation and interview. You will not always be informed about the exact nature of the assessments and this is in order to be able to accurately compare across a cohort of student applications in terms of ability and experience. Ultimately it is important to prepare for any interview or assessment day and to be ready to answer questions from the course team. Remember that this is also your opportunity to ask questions about the course and options for research.

There are occasions where students are rejected either at the stage of application or at interview / assessment and this can occur for a number reasons including that the candidate has an inappropriate and/or naïve conception of the role of forensic psychology, does not have relevant experience or does not have an appropriate understanding of the requirements of the course. Supportive references are also sought from nominated referees.

Being a student on a MSc Forensic Psychology course

The experience of being a student on an MSc Forensic Psychology course is really what you make it. Courses are run where full time students attend two days a week completing the equivalent to four modules (120 credits) over the course of two terms / semesters and part time students complete two modules (60 credits). The thesis / dissertation (60 credits) is therefore completed either over one or two years. Lecture attendance is a requirement of the course from the British Psychological Society and therefore registers are taken. The assignments completed on the MSc are designed to assess student knowledge and develop relevant skills, which can be implemented during practice training in Stage 2. Furthermore, lectures vary from traditional teaching and discussions to workshops and practice debates. Depending on the course, students can develop traditional and practice focused skills with academic essays and exams, individual and group presentations, report writing (expert evidence and risk assessment), case formulation, court observations and negotiation. The three weekdays that are not designated as lecture time are assigned to independent study and also provide students with time to develop and work on assignments and their research.

Many of the MSc courses available have external speakers who teach in their specialist area. This is not only a fantastic opportunity to hear people with practice experience discuss the cutting edge of the field of forensic psychology but also allows students to make good contacts and network. The field is competitive for employment opportunities even following the completion of an MSc and therefore a discussion during a lecture can help students to stand out when applying for jobs later down the line.

Thesis / Dissertation

The research you conduct at postgraduate level should be viewed as a requirement of your course but also an opportunity to develop your experience and research portfolio and to gain links with practitioners working in applied forensic settings. When considering the topic area you also need to think about the staff on the course that are available to supervise and their particular areas of research. In terms of your own professional development, you might want to think about whether you want to conduct research in the ultimate area you are interested in, if you want to develop and further undergraduate research (depending on relevance) or to conduct research in a completely different area to gain broader experience.

Depending on whether you are undertaking the course on a full or part time basis, you will need to write an application for ethical approval which may only be required within the university or via an electronic process such as the IRAS which is used for

NHS and prison / probation research. This is a good experience and particularly if you want to work as a forensic psychologist or remain in an academic environment because you will learn the processes for developing a proposal and gaining access to a particular participant sample. It is important to develop viable proposals that can be achieved in the time you have and to aim to pursue the research beyond the MSc. This means considering writing up the research for consideration in a peer reviewed journal publication and to present the research at a relevant conference. The main conference in the UK, which is student friendly and relevant to this field, is the British Psychological Society Division of Forensic Psychology Annual Conference. This is a further opportunity to understand what else is going on in the field and to get to know others in the area.

So what are your prospects on completion of the MSc Forensic Psychology?

It is easy to believe that once you have the MSc under your belt that an entire host of opportunities will present themselves to you. Unfortunately this is much more of an ideal perspective than a realistic one. You have to remember that although you have an MSc, so do many other people who are in the same position and therefore it is critical to stand out from the crowd. So, how is that possible? The main thing I can suggest is to ensure that throughout your studies you are engaging in personal development, volunteering, and becoming a rounded individual who can fit into working with a multidisciplinary team environment. There are opportunities although it might be that you need to travel to or live in an entirely different part of the country. If you are flexible, you will find that the options are much greater. Living somewhere else for the purpose of getting experience is well worth it.

The options available following an MSc really depend on whether you have decided to follow the route to forensic Chartership or want to become a Clinical Psychologist and apply for the D.Clin.Psy. course, which is offered at a range of Universities around the country. If you decide on the option of completing Stage 2 towards Chartership in forensic psychology then you need to opt for one of three routes; (i) obtaining employment as an Assistant or Trainee Forensic Psychologist; (ii) undertaking a top-up qualification to gain a D.Foren.Psy., or (iii) undertaking the Stage 2 process independently.

Historically, the main route has been to attain employment as either an Assistant Psychologist or a Trainee Forensic Psychologist. Both of these jobs are still relevant although the competition for posts can be fierce. So you need to think about whether you want to work in a secure setting such as a prison or hospital or in the community. It is not only the NHS or the Prison Service who advertise for posts here. Look also at the private sector because there is a range of opportunities there where you could work in a private hospital or prison. It is all about thinking away from the norm. It might be that in the first instance that a job won't provide you with the opportunity to complete Stage 2 but that in time you will be able to apply for a post internally within the organisation where you are employed.

The second option is a relatively new one and requires remaining a student and completing a professional doctorate in forensic psychology (D.Foren.Psy.) course as a top-up option for two years (or if you do not have an MSc Forensic Psychology, as a full three year doctorate). This course leads to a practitioner doctorate, chartership with the British Psychological Society and Registration as a Forensic Psychologist with the Health Professions Council. The requirements to be accepted onto the top-up courses are not just that you have completed successfully an MSc but also that you have gained a specific amount of practice experience working in relevant settings. The information about the work required to complete this option is available online and at present the Universities offering these courses are Birmingham and Nottingham.

The final option, which is perhaps the more challenging of the three, is to complete your Stage 2 Chartership independently. This has been an option taken up by academics teaching at Universities and others who work in a forensic setting but don't have the exact role of that mentioned in the first route. If you decide to take this option, you will need to ensure that you are working in a forensic setting and gain advice from the DFP of the British Psychological Society so that you can work toward the completion of the various core roles and submit your exemplars. This route will require you to identify someone who can act as the Co-ordinating supervisor and it is likely that you will have to pay for supervision sessions with them. The DFP website contains all the information regarding the requirements for Stage 2 and therefore will assist in making the decision whether to complete the requirements independently.

The above three routes are really for those people who have made the decision that they would like to work in practice as a "Forensic Psychologist". If you decide that the MSc Forensic Psychology has provided a good background in the field but that you don't want to become a practising psychologist, then there are other options open to you. It might be that you have really enjoyed the research aspects of your undergraduate and postgraduate courses and feel that completing a PhD in an area of forensic psychology would be of interest. This might ultimately lead to you becoming an academic and teaching future students in the field.

You might decide to work in an area aligned to Forensic Psychology where you still work in forensic settings such as becoming a Probation Officer, Prison Officer, Police Officer, Customs and Immigration Officer. These jobs all provide different opportunities but do all result in working with offending populations. If you are more interested in the investigation of crime and want to work in that area, the options for psychologists are limited. However you might want to consider applying to the police and ultimately working in CID as a detective. If you feel your skills are much more analytical, then there are options to work as a crime analyst either within a regional police force or nationally within the Serious Crime Analysis Section (SCAS) which is part of the National Policing Improvement Agency (although it is moving to another section within Government), the Research and Statistics section of the Home Office or working for the Serious Organised Crime Agency (soon to become the National Crime Agency).

Ultimately there are many options available post-MSc although not all of them are going to take you directly to becoming chartered. Keep your options open and take opportunities if they come your way even if they are not exactly what you were intending to do. In this field it is the experience that counts and the ability to not just want to be a Forensic Psychologist, but a *good* Forensic Psychologist!

*"**John**" now provides an account of how he developed an interest in forensic psychology. He also offers an opinion on the difference between forensic psychology and clinical psychology.*

So how did I become a forensic psychologist? Well if we are going right back to the beginning I actually wanted to be a hand surgeon. When I was doing my A-Levels, pretty much that's what I was going to do. But then it turned out that competition was too tough to be a medic, and I was left in a position where, because I'd applied to medical school and nothing else, then when I didn't get a place I had a year to, kind of, think about what I wanted to do. And it really was a case of reading different material; I don't know where the interest comes about wanting to try and make a difference but it seemed to me that this was another way that I could say to myself... "Okay if I can't get into medicine there's still the possibility of making some kind of a difference, by studying psychology". So I applied for psychology and physiology and I got offered two places; I went to Southampton. And then when I finished at Southampton I assumed that, when you finish university that everyone just messes about for several years, you know, [Chuckle] and so I spoke to some of my friends, saying, "So what, you know, what are you going to do when we've all graduated?" And I was amazed because one person had got a job lined up and one friend was going off to do a Master's degree and one was going off to do a PhD and there's all these, kinds of, things, so I thought, "oh right I've completely misunderstood how life progresses". So I applied for a Master's degree at the Ergonomics Unit in London. I applied for a job with ITT and applied for a PhD at Cambridge. The ITT thing, it was to do human factors; so man-machine interface stuff and I went along and had to do all these tests and I had about three days of tests and being put up at a fancy hotel and then I got to meet the psychologist and he said to me, "Yes, we haven't got a job for you, we just thought it'd be interesting to meet you." So you're, kind of, oh great!

Then when I went to the Master's interview, it was all going fine and I had the final interview with two interviewers one sitting in front of me and one sitting behind me. Someone would ask me a question and I'd be answering that and before I'd finished the other person would ask me a question. So I, sort of, turned round and I was doing this, kind of, weird turning round thing trying to please both of them, which I think is a good lesson; don't try and please everybody. And they said at the end of the interview, "Is there anything that you want to ask?" So I said, "Yes, is this the way you interview everyone because I can't believe anyone would come along to your course if this is the way you treat them?" So, they offered me a place but without funding; then there was the PhD; it was at the Medical Research Council's (MRC) Applied Psychology Unit and they offered me a place with funding so that's why I ended up there. I was doing stuff with Phil Barnard and that was very much, kind of, human-computer interaction stuff. But the work I was doing was more about learning and decision-making and at the time Phil has got this model, Interacting Cognitive Subsystems, and he was beginning to apply that more towards emotional issues rather than interacting with machines. So I was already beginning to think about, "well okay are these ways we can understand behaviour?" I think then I actually started to focus on the thought "I want to understand why *this* person does this and *that* person doesn't".

So then (after the PhD) I went to complete post-doctoral work in California with Don Norman and again I was exposed to an awful lot of the different kinds of things, like I was introduced to the world of parallel processing, stuff that was big over there at the time and tonnes of different disparate bits of information. After that I worked in Norway and I was lecturing in Cognitive Psychology and what happened was, that I'd just got really interested in the, decision-making material; in how people might try and conceal things and keep secrets. To me it seemed quite seminal stuff by a guy called Wegner. There's this whole thing going on about keeping secrets is more cognitively demanding and that's why actually it leaks out a bit because you've got less (cognitive) resources to do other stuff or to monitor your behaviour. So I got interested in that and I did a few simple studies, looking at people being secretive and being deceptive and got some interesting results from that. And then it was, kind of, this extension where I just started to think about, "well hang on a minute okay, so there's something about... seems to be something about being deceptive and of course, deception you, kind of, think about offending behaviour". And then I just got really interested in it and thought alright, "would I find the same kind of patterns in other kinds of offending?" And I got really interested in whether there was cognition of rape. Now being in Norway they've got a slightly different system where you are only a psychologist if you've done the clinical training programme and their view at that time was that if you've not done their clinical programme, you're not a psychologist and if you're not a psychologist, you can't collect data on people. So I was actually not allowed to do this piece of research that I really wanted to do. So what I did was, that's why I decided to go and do the Masters in Forensic Psychology in Surrey; so I took a year out of work.

I went and did that and then made, probably the worst decision I've made in my life, and I then went back to Norway for, as it turned out, it was only for a year. Thinking at the time that now that I had this extra degree (MSc in Forensic Psychology) which, kind of showed that I'd done some learning and I understood things, that they would say "Okay, yes". But still they said, "No, sorry, you know, you've got a BSc, you've got a PhD, you've got an MSc, it doesn't count". So I, kind of, went well, "Screw you guys". So I came back to the UK and I was offered a job working with Peter Kinderman in Liverpool on a project to do with personality disorder (PD) and violence and when I moved up here to the north-west, that's when I met James McGuire and he's got connections with everyone, all over the place and because of having done the Master's and wanting to do the kind of research that I wanted to do I, kind of, pestered him a bit about, "All right, well where can I go and get some access". And through that I got an honorary contract with the Mersey Forensic Psychology Service. And that's where an awful lot of my research now... it isn't necessarily based there, but it's, kind of, being in that environment where the ideas get developed. It's through my connection with the Mersey Care Trust that I was able to get chartered as a forensic psychologist and here I am!

And so, that is a potted history of how I got to this stage in my career. So I think my initial interest in psychology was more in the field of ergonomics. Rather than really thinking about man and machine it was, "I'm really interested in this idea of, what, in America, they refer to it as "Situated Cognition". So that the idea that the way that you think is going to be biased or influenced by, not only what you're doing, but the environment that you're doing it in, and there's this whole idea that actually cognition doesn't happen in your head; it happens when you communicate and that could be by interacting with things, or talking to people, because the ideas are then, out. They're not in my head or your head, it's only by that shared space, where you know what I'm thinking; where I know what you're thinking. And it's more of that, kind of, thing about how stuff impacts upon the way that we interact. And I think that's why, although it seems like it's quite a large conceptual leap to go from thinking about a human computer interaction, to thinking about why people offend against children, in the sense that it is this situated thing within that context, that I don't think it is quite such a big leap.

I've got two roles now. I guess the primary role, because I'm not a clinical person is the research aspect; so primarily I lecture to the Year One trainees on the Clinical Psychology Doctorate programme. I also supervise trainees through the whole three years and I facilitate the forensic module of the clinical course; this is in year three. In the forensic module I teach about sexual offending, violent offending, personality disorder; also multi-professional issues. I really try and impress upon the trainees that they are working in a multi-systemic fashion. So, for example, there's you and the individual that you're working with but that might be within the context of probation and social services and it might be in the context of police and their family and their children and so and so forth. So I bring in people from social services, bring in people from probation, bring in people from the police, from Resettle, which is a Personality Disorder service for people in Liverpool. I think it's important that not only do trainees get the theory behind, say, aggressive behaviour, but also that they have a sense of "okay, they are *people*, they are *not* aggression; they're people and then thinking about well, all right, so what's going on in their lives that you have to take account of when you're trying to work with them". So, trainees need to know that professionals aren't working in isolation with the actual offender but the environment within which they operate as well, such as the probation service and the police.

I suppose for me it is this idea that there are different competencies but there are also different responsibilities with other professionals. With those different responsibilities and competencies, there are different ways of conceptualising the person and I do think that the way the psychologist thinks about the individual is going to be different from the way that the social services person conceptualises an individual and the way that the police do. They're trying to fulfil different roles and because of that I think there is pulling in different directions that I think psychologists need to be aware of this because they are going to get people phoning up and saying, "Okay we need you to do this", or "Why haven't you done that", or "This is what we're doing". And it may not fit with the way that they either think of themselves or they think of their role or they think of the individual. So I think it's important that they are, kind of, exposed to this, kind of, stuff in, I guess in the safe environment of university and training, where it is just, kind of, being exposed to it rather than being stuck in the middle of it and suddenly finding that you've got social services saying, "Well, yes, but we're taking the children away". And you're thinking, but what's going to be the impact on the person I'm working with if you say you're taking the children away and their engagement with what I'm trying to do.

I know that you want my opinion on how forensic psychologists may differ from clinical psychologists in conceptualising a problem. Well it's interesting because I would say that there should come a point when, no, there would be no difference because if we believe in the idea that you can get to the point where you can get a useful, *you won't necessarily get the right understanding*, but a useful understanding, that can have an impact on someone. You would hope that other psychologists would reach that same conceptualisation so that the same progress can be made. But I think there are differences and what I think is it comes from the knowledge base that the individual has and this is where I think there's an important difference. So for example, if let's suppose I was seeing a man with a forensic history. I would be expected to go to work with that person and come up with a formulation (hypothesis about why he offends and what maintains this offending behaviour), and then come up with some plan for them. But if they had something else going on at the same time, let's suppose they had an eating disorder then I would not say that I would be able to do anything with that eating disorder. And what we'd have to do is, we'd have to come up with some understanding; do the things need to be examined together? Does the eating disorder impact upon the work I'm trying to do? Is the work I'm going to do going to impact on the eating disorder? So, I think about what is best for this person; should I refer them to a clinical psychologist first?

Now where I think that's different is that someone who has trained as a clinical psychologist may have had some specific training in working with the individual who presents with the eating disorder. This may be their specialism. The difficulty I think is that until you reach a certain level in the profession, and this is true for forensic psychology as well as any other applied psychologist, it's like, well, okay actually at what point are you competent in both of those things to be able to make that judgement? And that's what I think is maybe, something of an issue; when you are a competent forensic psychologist, that's what you've focused on. Whereas I think it's possible that within clinical psychology, you may have a broad experience of a lot of things but maybe you don't have the same focus on the forensic aspects. That isn't meant to be saying that forensic psychologists are better at doing forensic work. What it is saying is that it depends on your skills. If you are a clinician and you are highly skilled in forensic then there is that… then, you know, great. It's all about having appropriate skills, appropriate knowledge and appropriate experience. But I suppose one of the big differences between the clinical and forensic work is that forensic is really, really, very boundaried. The way I think about it is that, at no point would I expect that either I or anyone else would think that it would be reasonable for me to work with a person with an eating disorder. Whereas clinical is this vast, vast area and you can imagine that it really encompasses, potentially anyway, applied psychology such as Occupational, Sports, Counselling, Forensic and Educational. I suppose that's the thing; well okay you have a broad range of experience but at some point maybe the crucial thing is, is it enough? Should a clinical psychologist go and work with for example sports people, if they have not really specialised in that area? It's really what you specialise in after your core training. Even when you're chartered, it's still that thing about you're constantly trying to learn for yourself, trying to learn through your colleagues and, you know, through people in the clinical team; all of my forensic work is done within a clinical environment; they're all clinical psychologists and I learn an enormous amount from working in that environment. So, I mean, I find it very positive to have that shared working environment of forensic and clinical.

I'll tell you about some of the destinations that my clinical trainees have moved on to after completing the doctorate. One of them very recently has just got a job in a medium secure service in the south of England; there's someone else who, I suppose it isn't strictly speaking forensic, but it's a Personality Disorder service. Someone else went to work in Broadmoor; another went to work in Ashworth Hospital; someone else has applied to work at Rampton. So yes, qualified clinical psychologists certainly get jobs in forensic environments. There's special hospitals really and PD units and secure units. I'm not aware of anyone graduating in Clinical Psychology here who has gone on to work for the prison service as a psychologist.

In the following chapter two forensic psychologists in training share their perspectives on their career to date and their ongoing work in order to gain chartership. Both are employed by HM Prison service but in different roles in different prisons.

Chapter 10: Two psychologists currently in training

You can now read the accounts of two forensic psychologists in training who are currently employed by HM Prison service.

"Rebecca"

I haven't always wanted to be a forensic psychologist or even a psychologist. After enjoying psychology and sociology at A level I studied for a degree that covered a bit of everything in relation to human behaviour! Whilst it was a very interesting course it did not confer with the British Psychological Society (BPS) Graduate Basis for Registration (GBR). This essentially meant that if I wanted to study for an MSc or Doctorate in Psychology I would be unable to do so.

When I graduated I started looking for assistant psychologist jobs in the NHS but when the opportunity to go travelling around Asia and Australia arose I put that on hold. By the time I came back the majority of private and public sector assistant psychologist posts required applicant's degrees to have the GBR, something that was not a requirement a year earlier. The Prison Service however did not require applicants to their psychological assistant posts to have the GBR or even a degree! This did mean lower pay in comparison to the NHS posts at the time but it was a "foot in the door".

So although I knew by then I wanted to work in the field of psychology I "fell into" forensic psychology. I spent about six months looking for positions (forensic or otherwise) but was limited as I wasn't too keen on moving around the country due to personal circumstances and lack of relevant posts out in the sticks where I live were few and far between. I rarely got responses let alone interviews and when I did enquire employers referred to large numbers of applicants. I did manage to get an interview for a psychological assistant post with a private healthcare provider but when speaking to fellow applicants realised that I was at a disadvantage due to my lack of experience.

After a few months I was starting to think I would get stuck temping for the rest of my life! Two psychological assistant posts in the Prison Service then came up within my local area. Both applications were identical, with one I didn't even get an interview but the other I did. As mentioned I didn't have any experience of working with forensic clients and any potentially relevant experience that I did have had a more clinical focus (working on a semi-secure unit for individuals with mental health problems and volunteering as a support worker for an eating disorder charity). What stood in my favour was doing my research into the role which enabled me to adapt and develop my understanding of the psychological theory behind what is typically the main role of psychological assistants; delivering offending behaviour programmes. This included an appreciation of the cognitive behavioural approach that such programmes tend to take and the "What Works" literature. I can't remember exactly what the topic of my presentation to the interview panel was, something to do with how to solve a problem I think. I do recall looking into some of the key aims and methods used on the Enhanced Thinking Skills (ETS) programme, a course that I was aware was delivered within the establishment at the time. The feedback following a (successful) interview was that despite my lack of experience they were impressed with my style of delivery and knowledge of relevant methods that would support facilitation of offending behaviour programmes.

I know that some will argue that whilst competition for posts was fierce then it doesn't compare to what it is like for graduates applying now. Experience is one of the best ways to show a potential employer that you are right for the job however I was recently involved in recruiting for a psychological assistant post, in the prison that I currently work in, and the individual that was selected had no experience with a forensic population. After completing a psychology degree she had ended up in auditing for a couple of years and was desperate to get out. What she lacked in specific experience she made up for in how she had developed key skills in a different environment. Recruitment in the prison service is competency based so unless you shoe horn your experience into your answers to the questions on your application form the interview panel don't even see the list of places where you have previously worked. Skills such as communication, being positive towards rehabilitation of offenders, coping styles, developing yourself and others, and skilfully persuading and influencing are seen as qualities that are just as important as experience.

So after joining the Prison Service in 2005 I secured some funding through their further education and training scheme to complete a conversion diploma in order to achieve the GBR. I did this through two years of part time study with the Open University and received some support from the Prison Service with study leave. When this was all done and dusted I had been a psychological assistant for approximately four years. I then applied for a role as a forensic psychologist in training that had fortunately come up at the establishment, which I was working in. At this time I was very much in two minds about whether I wanted to continue with this career choice. A number of trainee psychologists had been working towards Chartership for several years and making little progress. The task in front of me seemed to be a lot of work and it was quite disheartening that friends from University were a lot further forward in progression through their careers. However I enjoyed my job and had received some really positive feedback from managers about my suitability for continuing in the field. This included an awareness of a range of clinical issues when discussing cases, good organisational skills and an effective treatment style in delivering interventions with offenders. It made me realise that it was the right choice for me and I was determined to learn from where things had gone wrong for others.

As a trainee psychologist I went on to complete Stage 1 of the Qualification in Forensic Psychology (exams and a piece of research) which is now obsolete. I had wanted to do an MSc because I preferred a more structured way of studying however within the region that I worked this was not an option that was funded. I did think that if I had done a degree with the GBR and completed a forensic psychology masters straight afterwards I could have saved quite a lot of time. That's the beauty of hindsight!

Whilst completing Stage 1 of the qualification I remained in the category C prison where I was originally employed treatment managing the CALM (Controlling Anger and Learning to Manage It) programme. My role involved supervising facilitators and monitoring videos of sessions that they facilitated in order to give them feedback on their practice. I was also heavily involved in assessing suitability of offenders for the programme, delivering the sessions myself and writing post programme reports. At the time I line managed six members of staff (Prison Officers, Psychological assistants and Administration Officers). Whilst I sometimes felt my time could be better spent it was useful to gain experience in managing others in a variety of ways and it felt that this meant I was more respected within the department and establishment. As part of my role I also had input into the selection process for offenders entering the establishment's Therapeutic Community and assisted in the administration and interpretation of psychometric assessments.

Shortly before finishing Stage 1 of the qualification I moved to another category C establishment where I am treatment managing the Core Sex Offender Treatment Programme (Core SOTP) and will soon start delivering the Healthy Sexual Functioning Programme. I am line managing less staff and only those who will benefit more directly from my experience (two psychological assistants). This has meant that aside from treatment and line management I have been much more involved in completing a range of different risk and need assessments for offenders. I work predominantly with sexual offenders but have also gained experience in the areas of domestic violence, schema therapy, personality disorder, psychopathy and cognitive functioning.

So although it's taken me a little while to start what was known as 'Stage 2' of the Qualification in Forensic Psychology my experiences thus far have on the whole been very positive. The variety of my work has been great and I've had so many different opportunities to develop whilst working for the Prison Service from attending a wide range of training courses to being involved in local and national projects. I am also able to train others in the use of two key risk assessment tools for use with sexual offenders and regularly liaise with a variety of staff, both within my establishment and more widely.

I know that some people have not had such a positive experience but I would say that there have been some really important changes over the past few years to enable trainee psychologists who are starting the route to be better supported.

I started on the new route in 2011. Although I have not submitted any exemplars for assessments I have completed two of the four and I am currently halfway through the third one. The main problem with getting the exemplars submitted has been the time to collate the work that I have done and get it in a presentable format. I have had several opportunities for core role work come along at once and therefore have been onto the next bit before I have even finished the last! It would be really satisfying to have some work submitted and passed but I feel positive that I have completed a large part of the work (fingers crossed for me please!). A goal for the rest of the year will be to complete my third Core Role and have submitted all three for assessment. If I am able to complete all my work by next year it will have been eight years from gaining my first postgraduate psychology job to becoming a chartered psychologist.

My ability to give advice is limited to the fact that I have not received feedback on my submitted work thus far however I do have a number of tips that either I wish I had realised at the start or that have really helped me.

My key tips:

Take the time to get really familiar with the handbook, core role competencies and paperwork that you need to complete in order to gain chartership. Get as much advice as you can from other trainees. The Division of Forensic Psychology (DFP) forum is really useful to share experiences and of course network with other trainees in your establishment or region.

Don't start the route until you are ready. Initially I was frustrated with the time that it took for me to start the qualification, however, now I don't feel like my time in a psychological assistant post was wasted; it really prepared me for what was to come given that I didn't have experience in the field prior to that point. I feel much more confident in my practice and believe that gaining a good depth and breadth of experience should not be underestimated.

Keep your practice diary up to date, I CANNOT STRESS THIS ENOUGH! Make sure you use that half hour at the end of each day to fill it in as back tracking is such a pain. The same applies for competency logs. Update them once a week and take them to supervision regularly.

Protect your time. I have often been a bit of a people pleaser and that means that the things that are a priority to me, but less so for others, are pushed back. The harsh reality is that if you want to move through the route quickly you will find that you need to put in some extra hours; however I have found that if you make good use of your time and keep up to date the qualification is less likely to take over your life!

Don't submit enormous exemplar plans….you may be giving yourself more to do than you actually need. There's no harm in seeing if a plan will get approved.

Be pro-active. Set yourself goals and stick to them. You may find that some supervisors/ managers will really push you but sometimes you could feel less pressure and you will be working on your own a lot. Having self-motivation is the key!

I've been lucky in finding a co-ordinating supervisor who has a lot of experience and who I get along with really well. It's very rare that you get a choice on who your supervisor is but I would say that getting over any feelings of being intimidated by their status is key! You need to be able to share your concerns and say exactly how you feel in order to make meaningful progress through a route that has many challenges along the way. I would also suggest networking as much as possible. Most supervisors will admit that they are not experienced in all areas so if you have links with others who can support your learning (without treading on anyone's toes!) it can really help. After all, your supervisor has a specific role and sometimes we can place too many expectations on them rather than place the responsibility on ourselves!

"Lisa" is another forensic psychologist in training and here is her account:

In comparison to a number of contributors I have always wanted to pursue a career in psychology. My interest in crime and psychology began at an early age and I chose my A-Levels not on the subjects that would necessarily allow me to achieve the best grades but subjects that would aid me in the completion of a psychology degree. As a consequence I probably made life that bit more difficult for myself and I remember heated arguments with my parents over my choice of subjects. When choosing my university I did a large amount of research to ensure that all the universities I applied to confer with the British Psychological Society's (BPS) Graduate Basis for Registration (GBR). Even if you are not sure whether you want a career in psychology, thorough research at this stage will potentially save you time and potentially money in the future.

On finishing university I had secured work in a bank where I was offered the opportunity for training and progression however I knew this wasn't for me and had already begun applying for HM Prison Service vacancies within the Yorkshire and Humberside area. Other contributors have spoken about letters of rejection and this was also my experience. I remember my first application, I thought I had sold myself well demonstrating my motivation and desire for the job; however I received a letter stating I had not been successful and felt quite devastated at what I saw as my failure. I contacted the area office for feedback who informed me that there was in fact a structure to competency based applications; what the experience was, what you did and what the outcome was. It is essential to seek feedback following applications or interviews; I have found this has been invaluable to me enabling me to address areas of weakness as well as promoting areas of strength. I applied the feedback to my subsequent applications and was successful in gaining interviews and two offers of a position. The competition for Psychological Assistant and Forensic Psychologist in-training positions continues to increase and from my experience I think it is fair to say that applications from candidates who have completed relevant work experience has also increased. Whilst my work in the bank was not direct work experience in the field of psychology it did give me the opportunity to work with people from a range of backgrounds, how to deal with difficult situations and develop my communication skills. On a positive note, HM Prison Service is now much more open to offering voluntary positions and I would advise those wishing to pursue a career in psychology to seek some work experience if possible. For one of my colleagues this led to her gaining both a psychological assistant post and a Forensic Psychologist in-training post. Candidates should also consider why they want to be a psychologist; whilst interviewing work experience candidates I have frequently heard "I want it be like Cracker"...whilst this may be true have you researched what a forensic psychologist does?

I gained my first position as a Psychological Assistant in the High Security Estate within the Enhanced Thinking Skills team. Prior to gaining this post I was told that I could expect to be in the post for six months and then I would be ready for a Forensic Psychologist in-training post. However this was not the reality, as I have said competition for positions is fierce and I was in this post for two years. This was not however wasted time and whilst working within this team, I developed my interviewing skills, in particular motivational interviewing skills, my facilitation skills, my report writing skills and my time management skills. Furthermore as Psychological Assistants we were responsible for the administration and interpretation of IQ assessments. My experiences also confirmed to me this was definitely the profession I wanted to pursue and I decided to complete my MSc. There was no funding available nor was I able to reduce my working hours however I saw an advert for the University of Leicester's distance learning MSc in Applied Forensic Psychology in the *Psychologist* magazine, a publication of the British Psychological Society. I would recommend becoming a member of the BPS; it is a question (whether I was a member) I have asked and been asked in interviews. I applied for the MSc and was successful. In hindsight it may have been easier to undertake an MSc following completion of my undergraduate degree, however, as I have said I don't always take the easiest or most direct route and having been in education since the age of four I wanted and needed a break from study. The completion of my MSc was hard work but it allowed me to develop the habit of studying on my own and in my own time, essential skills when working towards chartered status.

During the first year of my MSc I secured a Forensic Psychologist in-training position in a Category B London establishment where I completed the final year of my MSc. To say this was a baptism of fire is an understatement. The prison held twice the number of men my previous establishment had and the target for ETS completions was double, staff sickness was rife and the environment was very different to the stable prison environment I had worked in previously. After an initial question of "what have I done" I embraced the experience and loved it. I became the Treatment Manager of ETS and then the Thinking Skills Programme (TSP). My role involved the delivery of the programme, supervising facilitators, their reports and monitoring videos of sessions that they facilitated in order to give them feedback on their practice. I also took on line management responsibilities, interviewed candidates for the positions of Psychological Assistants and Forensic Psychologists in-training, undertook the completion of the Needs Analysis for the establishment and developed staff training. I also undertook training in the Historical Clinical Risk 20 (HCR-20- violence risk assessment), Risk Matrix 2000 (RM2000), Structured Assessment of Risk and Need (SARN) and Psychopathy Checklist Revised (PCL-r). The training made available to me was diverse and varied and because there had not been many openings to undertake training as a Psychological Assistant I was eager to embrace every opportunity. Despite this having worked in the establishment for two years I made the decision to move on. Whilst I enjoyed the work I was very conscious of the need for trainees to have a breadth of experience in a variety of areas and felt that the establishment could not offer me this due to the amount of TSP needed to be delivered in order for the establishment to achieve their targets. Candidates should be aware that prisons are as target driven as any business and as a member of a team you will be expected to strive to meet those targets.

I then secured a second trainee position at a category C training prison again as the TSP Treatment Manager. When applying for trainee positions don't just apply because of the title, candidates should consider the nature of the role i.e. will you be a Treatment Manager, will you be involved in risk assessments, and consider the population and nature of offenders you will be required to work with and whether you have any personal barriers that may impact on your ability to do this effectively. The target here was smaller for TSP and as a consequence of this I have been able to reduce the time spent on both facilitation and management of the programme and more time applying the training I received in my previous establishment. I have been much more involved in completing a range of different risk and need assessments for offenders. I work predominantly with violent offenders and have gained experience in the area of domestic violence and also learning disability and cognitive functioning.

I have been a trainee for just over four years although I have only been registered on stage 2 for 20 months. There does appear to have been a sea-change in recent times with a definite drive to ensure that trainees are achieving chartered status and submission targets are now included on yearly appraisals. Furthermore working as regional psychological services is allowing trainees the opportunity to work outside of the establishment they are based in. I have recently developed and delivered attachment style staff awareness training to staff working in a YOI establishment for my core role 4a. I am also currently working on my core role 1a and 1b, core role 3a and 3b and core role 4b. I find the exemplars that follow a structured process and require you to prepare work for submission as you go along, for example the development and delivery of training easier to prepare for submission as opposed to less discrete pieces of work as it can be difficult to find time to compile work that you have completed and put it together to a presentable standard ready for submission.

As I and other contributors to this work have discovered, it is recognised and accepted that throughout the chartership process your competence, confidence and commitment will fluctuate and it is important to identify strategies to manage times where it is low because chartership is something that requires time and commitment both inside and outside of work. Despite all this I love the work I do and I wouldn't change any of the decisions I have made.

In the following chapter we hear from two very experienced psychologists who currently supervise forensic psychologists in-training.

Chapter 11: Perspectives from Forensic Psychologists supervising trainees

Louise Bowers provides a reflective account of her career and then offers insight into the relationship between the supervisor and the supervisee (FPiT).

"None of this was planned: I am an accidental psychologist"

This is probably not the best way to start a section in a book for individuals considering a career in forensic psychology - but it is true. I suppose I am fairly driven and determined (qualities readers of this book will require in bucket loads), but I have had some incredibly lucky breaks along the way, and I have had the honour of working with some truly inspirational forensic psychologists. However, the fact remains that I had no great plans to become a forensic psychologist, nor any other type of psychologist; it just happened!

I didn't put much thought into either my choice of university or degree. I applied to Sheffield University because I had visited my brother who was studying there and I liked it. I chose psychology because it sounded interesting and I had unfortunately chosen a strange combination of A levels that prevented me from undertaking many degree courses. I graduated in 1990, and then got my first lucky break, because where many of my fellow students were unemployed and filling their days watching daytime TV, I was immediately offered a job working at the university. The professor who had supervised my undergraduate thesis was looking for a research associate for a Medical Research Council funded study examining the family relationships of bullies and victims in inner city middle schools in Sheffield, and he offered me the job. I worked on this project for two years and published a few papers, but realised that if I wanted to remain in academia I needed to complete my doctorate and I wasn't sure I was ready for this.

Lucky break number two came as I was discussing my dilemma over coffee one day with a colleague. She showed me an advert in *The Guardian* for fully funded trainee forensic psychologist posts with The Prison Service; a position I had not heard of before. I thought it sounded quite interesting and applied, but I was not initially called for interview. However, I received a telephone call quite late one winter Friday evening from the Prison Service to say that there had been a cancellation for the assessment centre on the Monday morning and would I be interested in attending? I think that would classify as lucky break number three?

I was successful at the assessment centre and interview and lucky break number four came in being sent to train at HMP Wakefield, which at the time (1992) held a very high number of high risk prisoners with complex needs. HMP Wakefield also had the largest psychology team in the country, although this would be considered small by today's standards! My MSc degree in Applied Criminological Psychology at Birkbeck College (University of London) was fully funded by the Prison Service and I completed this in two years and was awarded a distinction overall. While I was training, I received superb supervision and support from a range of extremely experienced forensic psychologists, and was given the opportunity to engage in a wide breadth of work– something that many of my colleagues at that time were not fortunate to have.

Lucky break number five came when HMP Wakefield became a pilot site for the then fledgling Sex Offender Treatment Programme (SOTP) and I was fortunate to be trained as one of the first facilitators. My interest in working with sexual offenders was sparked and I completed my MSc dissertation on typologies of sexual offenders, under the supervision of the then national lead for SOTP. I was awarded Chartered Psychologist status in 1994, and was immediately transferred to Prison Service headquarters in London, to work at what was then called Offending Behaviour Programmes Unit (OBPU). At that time OBPU consisted of two psychologists and an administrative assistant. I feel honoured to have had the opportunity to work so closely with these two psychologists, whose research into the assessment and treatment of sexual offenders is renowned worldwide. The team soon expanded when we were set the task of developing and preparing the suite of sex offender treatment programmes for accreditation. I was also involved in the original development of Risk Matrix 2000 (RM2000) and the structured assessment of risk and need (SARN).

Whilst I was working at OBPU I had two children and also went on secondment to HMYOI Feltham. Both of these events sparked my interest in working with young people in the criminal justice system, and this has become my area of particular expertise. My final post in the Prison Service was as a senior manager at HMP Highdown, where I was responsible for one of the largest psychology and programmes teams in the country. I quickly realised that I was not cut out for senior management; I disliked giving bad news to my staff and I missed direct contact with prisoners too much. I left the Prison Service in 2002, and after a short period of reflection, I took a post with South West London and St George's Mental Health Trust, as a highly specialised forensic psychologist. I worked part time in Wandsworth Youth Offending Team (YOT), and also held cases in the Child and Adolescent Mental Health Service (CAMHS). This experience confirmed my belief that forensic psychology had a lot to offer young people who came into contact with the criminal justice system and this is where I wanted to practise.

Whilst working at Wandsworth YOT lucky break number six came along, in that, the Parole Board had decided to appoint a number of forensic psychologists for the first time. As the Prison Service no longer employed me I was eligible to apply. The recruitment procedures were intense and extremely demanding and I came away from the process thinking that if I had found it that difficult, this meant professionally I was probably not ready for a public appointment. However, I was in fact successful and was one of the first two forensic psychologists appointed to the board in 2003; something I am incredibly proud of. I spent seven happy years developing the role of forensic psychology on The Board, and during this time I was fortunate to be selected to sit on some of the highest profile and professionally demanding cases. I also had the privilege of being involved in the recruitment, training and mentoring of new members; something that I am still involved in today. My continuing links with the Parole Board are very important to me, and I am frequently commissioned to provide a range of specialist training and workshops using my experience from sitting on both sides of the table.

In 2005 my family left London and it was not feasible to commute back to Wandsworth to work but I continued to sit as a member of The Parole Board. I had planned to have another period of reflection, but I quickly became bored and so I decided to let a few solicitors know that I might potentially be available to take instruction.

Lucky break number seven was how quickly the work rolled in. I quickly secured far too much work for one person and a colleague and good friend soon joined me and we formed a partnership. In addition, an extremely competent forensic psychologist in training (FPiT) decided she would like to continue her training independently and fund this by taking on work on a self employed basis, and so she joined us too. The practice grew quickly, and in 2011 I and my partner decided to incorporate the business into a limited company, and so The Forensic Psychologist Service (Ltd) arrived. This practice is a little bit different than most, as, apart from engaging in the more obvious expert witness work for the Crown and family courts and the Parole Board, the company has been able to secure contracts with private providers of mental health and secure forensic services as well as the Prison Service, children's secure units and children's homes. We also see private clients and provide specialist training. In addition, we provide professional supervision and interim cover where forensic psychologist vacancies exist. This has ensured that we have all been able to continue to engage in a wide variety of work whilst at the same time maintaining a significant practice base. The reputation of the company has developed over the years, and we are now known for specialising in unusual, high risk and complex cases that are often also very high profile. The one FPiT who was associated with the company has now qualified and is currently on maternity leave, and we now rarely accept instruction for the types of straightforward case that a FPiT could take on. Consequently, we are not currently in a position to offer FPiT positions. However, the whole criminal justice system is in a state of transition currently and no one really knows what this will mean in the future for independent practices.

Most recently I was appointed as a partner to the Health & Care Professions Council (HCPC). This has given me an invaluable insight into what is perceived as safe, effective and ethical practice from the perspective of a regulator, as opposed to from within the profession. I have also been appointed to lecture on two university MSc level degree courses in forensic psychology and applied psychology. It is wonderful to have the opportunity to play a part in the education of the next generation of forensic psychologists. However, after every lecture I deliver, there is always a group of students who gather at the front of the room to ask about careers in forensic psychology, and more specifically how to gain the relevant experience that it seems is required to secure a FPiT position and / or a supervisor. I am therefore delighted that Brendan has written this book, and as competition for employment increases further, in my view it will become an invaluable resource for anyone thinking about embarking on a career in forensic psychology.

I have supervised Forensic Psychologists in-training (FPiT) for the past 15 years and through all of the different training routes approved by the BPS and more recently the HCPC. I am on the register of applied psychology practice supervisors (RAPPS), which is designed to recognize psychologists with special expertise in supervision. Although it is possible for psychologists who are not on RAPPS to still supervise

FPiT, I would always advise that, wherever possible, the FPiT should seek a supervisor who is on the register. It is perfectly acceptable for a FPiT to seek confirmation of this, and the BPS offer a register search facility. In addition, I am an assessor of Stage Two of the Diploma in Forensic Psychology, which means that I assess exemplars that FPiT submit when they are working towards chartership. Apart from being enjoyable work, marking exemplars gives me a helpful overview of what standards are required for FPiT to demonstrate competence across the four core roles. This is invaluable information, which I make good use of in my supervision sessions with the FPiT that I am the coordinating or designated supervisor for.

Providing professional supervision is the aspect of my work that I enjoy most. I take great pride in assisting with the professional development of the FPiT who I am currently supervising. Equally, I take a keen interest in the careers of the psychologists I have previously supervised through to chartership and professional registration, and some of them now occupy very senior and influential roles in the forensic world. I have supervised FPiT as part of my employment through private contracts with organisations who have decided to outsource this task and I have also supervised two FPiT who were taking the independent route to chartership. Reflecting on this, I have concluded that the nature of my role and responsibilities as a supervisor has been slightly different depending on the nature and context of my relationship with the FPiT.

In the earlier part of my career, when I was still employed by the Prison Service, I was required to supervise FPiT as part of my employment contract; I was also line manager for these same individuals. In my experience, line management is usually driven by organisational objectives; it is task focussed and unfortunately is often about getting the job done as quickly as possible. Whereas professional supervision is supposed to be more about the *process* of getting tasks done, and should therefore be a much more reflective process. I found combining these two roles difficult. The major issue was that supervision was often cancelled, postponed or condensed when organisational needs appeared to be greater or more urgent than the training needs of the supervisees. In addition, when supervision did occur it was too easy to focus on tasks and problems rather than processes and reflections. Unfortunately, in many organisations, particularly where there is only one registered psychologist in a particular unit or site, this remains the only way to organise things. However, I am aware that in the Prison Service some areas that have adopted the regional model have found a creative solution to this problem. In this situation, two qualified psychologists (who may work in different parts of the region) will share and separate out the responsibility for line management and professional supervision for a number of FPiT, and this seems to work well.

Since leaving the prison service I have been able to offer professional supervision to FPiTs either through contracts with individual organisations or directly to FPiT working towards chartership and registration independently. I consider that my role as supervisor is very different in this situation. I am paid a fee for supervision and expectations of rapid and successful completion of the Diploma in Forensic Psychology are high from both FPiT and senior managers who are paying for the contract. However, there are considerable advantages to this arrangement. For example, in these circumstances there is a choice about who is commissioned as supervisor, and so a psychologist who will best meet the needs of the FPiT at that stage can be selected. In my experience, sessions tend to be focused on work that will help the FPiT progress towards chartership rather than work that the organisation needs completing. In addition, supervision sessions taking place on a fee paid basis appear to be viewed as important by everyone concerned, and are rarely if ever cancelled.

Whatever the circumstances in which supervision is taking place, I take my role as practice supervisor extremely seriously. By definition, a trainee is not able to practice autonomously and so responsibility falls to the supervisor to ensure that the supervisee is given opportunities to develop professionally, whilst at the same time safeguarding the welfare of the client (which in my practice is usually a defendant, serving prisoner, or ex-prisoner), and protection of the public. This is sometimes a difficult balancing act, particular when, as has happened to me, I have been supervising FPiT who want to progress quickly and are requesting tasks that professionally, I do not consider they are yet competent to complete. This is often due to a lack of reflection on the part of the FPiT, and encouraging reflective practice is a key task of supervision. I have supervised FPiT whose primary goal is to achieve chartership as quickly as possible; these supervisees required a great deal of support and assistance with developing reflective skills. Equally, I have supervised FPiT who have become so reflective that they have been plagued with self-doubt about their abilities and competence. This situation has the potential to become a significant barrier to progress towards chartership and registration and has required me to encourage them to be much more task focused.

When I am supervising FPiT I try to combine and integrate three roles, which are, educator, provider of support and clinical oversight of work undertaken. Supervisors have to be flexible, and as FPiT develop in competence the balance of these three roles shifts. For example, the degree of education required often lessens as supervisees develop professionally, but clinical oversight sometimes increases as they begin to take on more complex cases. In addition, I have found that supervisees' need for support often fluctuates over the course of their professional development. This can be because they are asked to take on tasks or clients that they find extremely challenging, or sometimes because they are experiencing issues in their personal life that are having an impact on their work. Again, a good supervisor should be able to respond flexibly to these changing dynamics.

In my view, the nature of the relationship between the supervisee and the supervisor is critical to both the safe and effective practice of the FPiT but also to their chances of successfully gaining chartered and registered status. I believe that I put a great deal of effort into creating an environment where the individuals I supervise feel valued, understood and safe. In my view, creating this type of environment is vital if supervisees are to be able to honestly discuss the difficulties they will inevitably experience in the course of their training. However, I understand that being able to disclose when difficulties are arising or have already arisen can be difficult for some supervisees, because understandably, they are often anxious about how they may be judged. In addition to the other three roles, when I am acting as a coordinating supervisor, I also have an assessor role with responsibility for assessing if supervisees are competent to practice independently. I am aware that some FPiT may fear that if they discuss cases or tasks that are not going well, their career development may be hampered. On occasions, I have had to have these sorts of difficult conversations with supervisees, but in the world of forensic psychology public protection must always come before career progression.

I view supervision as a dynamic learning process, where both the supervisee *and* the supervisor learn and develop. I also consider that the supervisor and supervisee should share responsibility for maintaining a respectful working relationship that enhances learning. I do not work in a way where I 'give' supervision, and the supervisee 'receives' it, and I can honestly say that working in a more equitable way has meant that I have learned so much from the FPiT that I have supervised over the years. Whilst I appreciate diversity, in my experience, it helps if the supervisor and supervisee share a broadly similar set of values and beliefs. For example, despite sitting as a member of the Parole Board for seven years, I do not consider myself risk averse. I have a fundamental belief that most of the individuals I work with have a desire for and the capacity to change, and my role as a psychologist is to assist them in that process. Also, because I specialize in work with high-risk children and young people, I am constantly reminded of the influence of early experiences on later development. This has influenced my belief that even when working with adults, it is not possible to have an effective case formulation without taking the individuals' early experiences into account. FPiT who do not share these fundamental beliefs, or who were not willing to explore their own beliefs about these issues would probably find supervision with me challenging.

In my view, many of the potential difficulties and stresses with the supervisor / supervisee relationship can be avoided by having a supervision contract; something I insist on. In such a contract, both the supervisor and supervisee can outline their expectations of the relationships and preferred ways of working and receiving feedback at the outset. They can also highlight how they will deal with any difficulties they may experience as supervision progresses and what the contingencies are if the relationship breaks down completely, but in my experience this is extremely rare.

In my opinion, all psychologists who are supervising FPiT should engage in both a comprehensive range of continuing professional development activities and some form of supervision. To be able to take on the role of educator in the supervision relationship, it is vital that supervisors keep abreast of developments in the field. I tend to set annual personal CPD goals for myself. So, for example last year, I set a goal to read at least one peer reviewed journal article per week, and this year I am applying to complete a doctoral top-up course. This is in addition to attending training events and conferences. As a supervisor you are clinically responsible for not only your own work and decision-making, but also that of the individuals you supervise. I have found this a heavy burden to bear at times, particularly as I spend quite a lot of time working in isolation. At these times, I have found contact with my peer supervision network vital to me being able to maintain my well being. My company also engage in regular case and report reviews with peers, and this provides not only a route to supervision but also a degree of governance that is vital in the current climate.

As psychologists progress through their careers and find the areas of work that really interest them, it is inevitable that they become more specialised. This means that when they are supervising FPiT they may not be practicing and fully competent in all areas that the supervisee will be assessed in. For example, some supervisors are academics who tend not to conduct many assessments or interventions. Equally, some supervisors are full time practitioners and may not have time to conduct research. In my view, it is vitally important that supervisors are aware of the limits of their competence in terms of their own current practice and are able to communicate this honestly to their individuals they are supervising. The BPS and HCPC recognize that experienced and senior psychologists cannot always maintain a high level of competence in all key work areas, and so there are provisions for FPiT to be provided with "designated" supervisors for specific pieces of work. Personally, I welcome this approach as it provides the potential for FPiT to be exposed to a broader range of experience and excellence.

Someone once said that "things work out best for those who make the best of the way things work out". This is certainly true of me. I have been presented with some incredible opportunities, and I have worked with some inspirational psychologists as my career has progressed. However, I believe that I seized every one of those opportunities and learned as much as I could from every person I have worked alongside. I fully acknowledge that becoming a forensic psychologist now is far more challenging and competitive than when I was starting out; I have seen how hard potential FPiT work at creating opportunities that will help them progress, rather than having opportunities presented to them. In my view, the individuals who succeed are extremely organized, tenacious and determined, and of course they have good supervisors! It is worth sticking at it, and for those of you that succeed in becoming a forensic psychologist you will have an incredibly rewarding career ahead of you; one that I would not change for the world.

Finally, **Kerry Manning** is a Registered Forensic Psychologist and has recently supervised two trainees through the process of successfully gaining chartership. Kerry manages her own company and has a number of qualified associates and members in-training working with her.

It was never my childhood ambition to become a forensic psychologist. Although I came from the *Silence of the Lambs* generation, where many of my female school friends had watched the film and vowed to become the next Clarice Starling, I was less decisive as a teenager. I think I was always keen on pursuing a career, which linked in with crime and law, but I had no concrete plans for further education or training. However, by the time I'd completed my GCSEs, I'd decided to join the police force. I think I was most attracted to the diverse job description such a position would bring; I was never one for routine and stability during my adolescence. How times have changed!

At that time, in the early 1990s, it wasn't possible to train as a police officer until the applicant reached the age of 18. I opted to study for some A levels while I waited to become eligible, although came close to getting a full-time waitressing job for an 18 month period instead to bide my time and earn a bit of money. It was never my intention to go to university, but once I had my A levels under my belt, I was suddenly presented with the possibility of leaving the Isle of Wight and living in a city for three years. Although my A level grades were fairly average, in September 1994 I began my BA with honours degree at the Liverpool Institute of Higher Education (now Liverpool Hope University College); affiliated to the University of Liverpool. I chose to study psychology, only because I thought it might come in useful when I eventually qualified as a police officer.

Once at University I began to develop a passion for psychology; a subject I'd had had very little exposure to before this time. In the first year of my degree, I was still keen to pursue a career in the police force and, by the end of the year I'd secured a position working as a Special Police Constable, stationed in Liverpool city centre. Quite a change from seasonal work at the seaside resort I had grown up in! As it turned out, my experience in the police was a major factor in me getting onto my forensic psychology MSc degree at the University of Surrey. Back in 1997, as I remember, there were only three universities offering BPS accredited forensic psychology MSc degrees, and so the competition was extremely tough. Although I was predicted a 2:1, it was my "real life" experience that got me onto the course and I would urge you to seek these types of experiences whilst studying in order to get ahead of your peers. It's not all about the grades you achieve. Psychology is about people, communication and interaction.

Getting back to 1995 - In my second year of study at Liverpool, I managed to arrange a work placement back on the Isle of Wight, working in the psychology department at one of the Isle of Wight cluster prisons. It was my experience here that shifted my career aspirations and by the end of my first degree I had decided to become a forensic psychologist.

In September 1997, I began my forensic psychology MSc degree at the University of Surrey. I had originally intended to complete the degree in a year. However, I was also working full-time throughout this period to support myself financially. By the end of the academic year, I wasn't achieving the standards expected as I had so little time to dedicate to studying and I had to make a very difficult decision; to admit defeat and pull out of the degree, or to accept the university's kind offer to allow me an additional year to complete my studies. After working a summer season back on the Isle of Wight and getting some much needed support from my parents, I embarked upon a second year at the University of Surrey and in the summer of 1999 I finally graduated.

Although I initially spent a few months working as a prison psychological assistant back on the Isle of Wight, I wanted to get back to the mainland and in 1999 I was offered a job as a basic grade psychologist at a Category C prison in Cambridgeshire. There was no structured route to chartership back then, nor any core competences to be demonstrated, although I worked under supervision for around two years before getting a job as a "Higher Psychologist" in a High Security prison (still in the Cambridgeshire area). It was here that I really matured and began reaching my potential under the supervision of a brilliant chartered psychologist, who completely inspired me, and in 2003 I was awarded chartered status. I spent the best four years of my life working at this establishment, both professionally and personally. The opportunities available in the prison service at this time were excellent, and I benefitted from a number of training and development opportunities. I was also extremely lucky to be part of a psychology team who were valued by prison management and considered integral to the day to day running of the prison.

However, all good things come to an end and in 2006 I moved up north to head up the Psychological Services department at a Young Offenders Institute (YOI). I had many exciting ideas about driving forward psychological services and raising the presence of psychologists in the establishment. Unfortunately, although my team were enthusiastic and shared my vision, the establishment had a different perspective on the use of psychologists in prisons and by May 2007, feeling rather disillusioned, I had made the decision to leave the prison service and set up my own private practice. Quite a risky and radical decision, especially since I'd just had my second son and now had two children under the age of two! I was also aware that, after reaching the Senior Psychologist grade, opportunities for further promotion became scarce, particularly if you were not prepared to relocate. As a mum of two young children, I no longer had the luxury of being able to move around the country so freely, and so independent practice seemed the perfect solution.

The creation of my company was an exciting and rewarding time for me. I learned quickly about networking, marketing and accounting and had built up a satisfactory caseload within a short time frame. I guess others in my position at that time might have struggled working alone for long hours, without the camaraderie you get with office-based teamwork. However, I embraced the peace and quiet when the boys were at nursery and began to enjoy my existence in the converted roof space of my house in Cumbria.

In December 2007, I moved back down to Cambridgeshire to be closer to family; relaunching the business in a more central location. It was at this point that I was offered a temporary contract supervising a small group of forensic psychologists at the high security prison I originally worked at, while they attempted to recruit a new head of unit. After four months of supervising and really enjoying the opportunity to help others gain focus and develop their skills once more, I began to make enquiries with the British Psychological Society as to whether I could take on and supervise my own group of psychologists in-training. Finally, in May 2007, my company doubled in size as my first associate joined the team. I'm not sure who was most anxious about the risks involved, but my first recruit is still working with me and is now a fully fledged registered psychologist.

I took on a further two psychologists in-training during late 2008 and early 2009 and, along with two chartered psychologists who joined along the way, our team was formed. Although we have gained and lost associates along the way, our core group has remained and we continue to enjoy peer support, team training, meetings and regular lunch dates! It has been a pleasure being part of a group who have all matured and developed so much since we got together, both within the team and through other commitments, pursuits, interests and academic ventures. I have to say that the supervision of psychologists in training has become one of the most important and rewarding aspects of my role over the past five years. I have been extremely lucky to have supervised three individuals who embrace feedback and development opportunities. They have also become very good friends. I'm not sure this always works in business and within a supervisory relationship, but it seems to have fallen into place for our team.

So, what works in supervision? I remember when I was supervising as a prison psychologist there was always a debate over whether it was best to keep supervision separate from line management and for different individuals to be allocated to each task accordingly. Personally, I always found it extremely useful to bring the two together; enabling the psychologist in training to actively plan to undertake core competences within their job role, facilitated and overseen by the supervisor. This is an approach I continue to take with my trainee associates, two of whom chartered this summer after embracing opportunities for training, consultancy and research around their core work in assessment and intervention. We have been extremely lucky to have kept in contact with a number of valued colleagues through both practice and academia; one of whom has acted as a designated supervisor for our associates in achieving competence in research.

Unless you are in a position where your employment provides a supervisor, I would recommend you try to find an individual with some understanding of the core roles and accompanying documentation, which needs to be submitted on a regular basis. Whilst I fully support the more stringent and competence based framework, which has developed since I became chartered, it is generally accepted that the accompanying paperwork can be a little complex and a strong supervisor might be more able to offer you guidance and shape your focus. They can also pester you to keep your practice diaries up to date! In my experience, it can be easy to drift along for some time, completing your core work tasks without sufficiently demonstrating each of the specific competences to practice independently. You'll need to work with your supervisor to create clear plans to complete tasks within structured, realistic timeframes. Not only will this make your work much more rewarding and fulfilling, it will also speed up the process of demonstrating competence, which, in turn, will offer financial benefits in the long-run. Maintenance fees are rather expensive if you are self-employed and responsible for funding this yourself. Also, be aware that, unless supervision is provided as part of your employment, it can be an expensive commodity, with some psychologists charging up to £100 an hour for their services.

As I mentioned, two of the psychologists in training I have supervised in my team achieved chartered status this year and are now registered with the Health and Care Professions Council (HCPC). As their supervisor, I knew they were ready to practice independently as our relationship became one of mutual support and learning. Essentially, these individuals were now taking responsibility for their own decision-making and clinical judgement without the need for excessive support and guidance from me, as their supervisor. My remaining original psychologist in training has also made exceptional progress and hopes to submit her last core role in summer 2013. I have also recently recruited another associate, who should qualify at around the same time and I'm very much looking forward to developing our supervisory relationship over the next year.

I guess my take-home message for those following a career in forensic psychology would be to take ownership of your own learning and development, keep focused and continue to set yourself achievable goals. A good supervisor will help you along the way, but ultimately you'll need your own drive and commitment to reach your goals. Also, remember that you'll never stop learning. Psychology is constantly evolving and we are continually embracing new theories that contribute to best practice. I believe I am learning and developing more now than I ever have done, despite having qualified almost ten years ago. This year, I am entering year four of a part-time PhD; something I never thought I'd be capable of in my younger years, and I am still learning so many new ways of working, writing and thinking to apply to my practice. I continue to find psychology a fascinating subject and hope I can continue to inspire others to feel the same for many years to come.

Chapter 12: Concluding comments

It is clear from reading the contributors' accounts that the earliest qualified forensic psychologists had greater opportunities for entering the career pathway than those that are graduating now. Some were very fortunate to be in the right place at the right time. Whilst it may seem odd to current graduates that a number of these psychologists (including the author) had originally never considered a career as a forensic psychologist we must place this information in context. There were far fewer MSc courses in forensic psychology, and prison psychology departments were smaller. Louise informs us that the SOTP suite of programmes was only developed in the 1990s so this helps us to understand why this career pathway has established itself so quickly since then. Many of the contributors to this eBook have told us about their role in facilitating on Offending Behaviour Programmes such as the SOTP.

So what have we learnt from the different accounts of the more recent trainees? Some people preferred getting an MSc prior to applying for jobs; others, perhaps through financial constraints, hoped that the employer would fund the MSc. We have heard mixed opinions about the type of work experience that is valued at interview and learnt that the real issue is being able to demonstrate in an application form and at interview how you apply your transferable skills to the forensic environment. We have also heard about the advantages and disadvantages of completing your training in the prison service or in hospitals. It would seem that a mixed approach would be ideal if that was possible; indeed this may be what is intended on the doctoral training route. Importantly, two contributors have urged you not to rush into roles before you are ready. Perhaps it is safe to conclude that there is more than one approach to accessing this career and that no approach is easy. It is vital though that you have considered all of these options, including exploring the other routes to training as a psychologist, and alternative careers with a similar client group, prior to investing time and money into this career pathway.

The chances are that many of you reading this text will have already experienced confusion and frustration at the lack of opportunities currently available to graduates interested in pursuing a career in forensic psychology. Undoubtedly, having the flexibility to uproot and move to where the few vacancies are is a bonus but of course this "luxury" doesn't apply to everyone. I hope that I have whetted your appetite for a career in forensic psychology whilst at the same time adding a realistic grounding about the effort required to gain a foot in the door of this career. In the same way that we cannot expect that everyone who achieves a good honours degree in psychology will become a psychologist, neither can we, in my opinion, expect everyone with an MSc in Forensic Psychology to become qualified forensic psychologists. This does not mean that all your effort and your knowledge has been wasted; rather you may need to consider alternative ways of applying the skills learned at undergraduate and postgraduate level to an alternative career choice. You may be one of the determined ones who knows the risks and will still go all out to succeed. Clearly some people do succeed! I hope that you feel a little more informed about this career choice and just as importantly that you have considered alternative careers in psychology or indeed in other associated careers. It was never my intention to dissuade you from this career choice but I sincerely believe that people need to be realistic about the financial challenges that may lie ahead and the impact that training may have on your leisure time. Those who are determined enough will hopefully find a way to succeed. As we have seen some people who started out very determined have chosen to change course after investing a lot of time, money and energy into training. Have you considered how you would cope with making that choice should your training environment not meet your expectations or your priorities in life change?

In summary, I have tried to explain in this book that it is not a simple case of gaining a good honours degree and walking straightaway into a trainee position. It really is **not** that simple. Competition for training places is fierce and they currently seem to be quite rare. Along the way you are likely to receive rejection letters. If you are prepared for these they might not be quite so painful. If you are determined to succeed I would encourage you to network widely. I have seen some graduates advertise their availability on LinkedIn profiles.

Top tips:

- Subscribe to the DFP Trainee Forum discussion group.
- Be proactive in seeking opportunities. They will not land in your lap.
- Have a Plan B.
- Ensure that you pay attention to spelling and grammar when making contact with potential employers. I have lost count of the number of graduates that write to me and spell my name incorrectly.
- Have a decent email address when contacting professionals. Nothing looks worse than a juvenile, macho or sexist **name@soandso.com**
- Network profusely. If you can afford to, try to attend relevant conferences and training days and speak to people there. The DFP run an annual conference.
- Gain relevant work experience and try to think through how you might be applying forensic psychology concepts and theories to your daily activities.
- Think laterally when looking for relevant work experience. Have you considered charities that assist with the resettlement of offenders or organisations that assist offenders who misuse substances?
- Do not compromise the final grade of your undergraduate degree: Aim for the highest marks that you can achieve, as this is what the competition is doing.
- If you have completed your accredited MSc and are independently seeking a supervisor for Stage 2 check the accredited supervisors register at the BPS.

At this point I just want to summarise a likely path that you may travel in your quest to become qualified. Firstly you need the BPS accredited undergraduate psychology degree. Some students find time to gain valuable *relevant* work experience during this period. Some graduates immediately commence an accredited MSc in Forensic Psychology whilst others gain relevant work experience in positions such as health care workers or assistant psychologists. Having gained work experience and possibly being in possession of an accredited MSc they may then seek out trainee posts. Trainee posts do seem to be rare these days though and certainly don't appear to be advertised very often in these times of public sector austerity. Remember to look for opportunities in the independent hospital sector as well as the prison service and the NHS. Some prisons are run by private companies. The Probation Service also employs forensic psychologists in some regions.

Hopefully, you now understand that if you want to be a Chartered Psychologist with the BPS and a Forensic Psychologist registered with the HCPC then you need to follow the BPS training route. As briefly noted though it may be possible to practise in the UK now as a non-chartered but Registered Forensic Psychologist by following a HCPC accredited training route such as that offered by Cardiff Metropolitan University. I cannot emphasise enough that you must access the HCPC and BPS websites regularly to keep informed of changes in accredited courses and training routes.

I have added a couple of recent job advertisements in the appendices that follow and then I have provided a list of some useful website addresses that may assist in your initial searches for relevant work experience. As I said at the outset I would appreciate any feedback that you have about this book and any ideas about how it may be developed. Perhaps before you go away to think further about this career you could complete a final task. Reflect on what your personal, work and academic strengths are that make you suitable for this career. Identify any weaknesses that you may have in your academic or work profile or indeed any aspects of your personality or life history that might make this a difficult career choice for you. What opportunities are currently available to embark on this career? Are you flexible in terms of location and would you really be prepared to move away from friends and family if offered employment elsewhere? Lastly, what obstacles are currently in the way of you achieving your goal, or may become obstacles in the foreseeable future? This little exercise might assist in giving some clarity to your thoughts.

Before you finish I want to introduce you to a few textbooks that should hopefully stimulate your ever growing interest in the field of forensic psychology. Firstly, a text book about psychology in prisons (Crighton & Towl, 2008), which has chapters discussing topics that include psychological assessments, violence and sex offending. Secondly, an introductory text book about psychological research in prisons (Towl, 2008), which introduces the reader to methodological issues and evidence-based research. If your interest lies more in the policing aspects of psychology such as profiling, crime analysis and court work then you might like to read a text about psychological profiling and criminal investigation (Alison, 2005). Finally, you may wish to consider *Forensic Psychology: Concepts, debates and practice* (Adler & Gray, 2010).

I wish you every success in your chosen career.

Appendix 1

Example job advertisement taken from the internet

Accessed on BPS Appointments page 17.07.12

Assistant
Psychologist
Employer:
Description: Responsible To: Director of Care

Hours of Work: 3 – 5 days per week by negotiation

Location: Gloucestershire

Deadline for Applications: Friday 20th July 2012
Interview Date: Tuesday 31st July 2012

Child & Family Services provide a range of specialist residential services for Looked After Children and Young People. The young people present with a variety of challenges requiring a flexible approach within a strong non-aversive, low arousal philosophy.

We currently require two Assistant Psychologists to fill vacancies in the Gloucestershire area. The successful candidates will be required to work independently, and must be willing to travel.

Applicants must have a BPS accredited degree in Psychology, and considerable post-qualifying experience in a care environment. An M.Sc. will be considered advantageous. In particular (for one post) we require a candidate with experience/interest in forensic work, to work with sexually harmful behaviours. Regular supervision will be provided by a Consultant Clinical Psychologist.

In return we offer childcare subsidy, loyalty bonus at 3 years+ and contributory pension scheme.

Working Hours: Full-time
Salary: Band 6, Pt. 22-25 (£24,831.00 - £27,844.00)
Location: South West
Closing Date: 20/Jul/2012

Author's comment: The salary offered for these private sector posts seems very good compared to many public sector posts that I have seen advertised. Look carefully at the above advertisement. If you were applying for this vacancy would you know how to define the term 'sexually harmful behaviour'? Would you consider reading some relevant research prior to applying?

Example job advertisement taken from the internet

Accessed on BPS Appointments page 17.07.12

Psychology Managers – Central Scotland Locations	
Employer:	Scottish Prison Service
Description:	The Scottish Prison Service is currently looking for full and part time Psychology Managers across a number of central Scotland locations holding a wide range of prisoners. The post holders will contribute to a range of functions performed by local psychology departments with an emphasis on the implementation of offending behaviour programmes and risk assessment and management, all of which contributes to the SPS aims of reducing re-offending and creating a safer Scotland.
	Full Time Posts (37 hours, permanent) : HMP Shotts, HMP Glenochil and HMP Barlinnie Part Time Posts: HMP Dumfries (29.5 hours)
	All candidates must hold a degree in psychology conferring Graduate Basis for Registration, and be qualified to post graduate level in forensic psychology or other relevant field. Being a Chartered or Registered Forensic Psychologist is preferable, however we will consider candidates who are registered for Stage 2 of the Qualification in Forensic Psychology or working towards registration as a Forensic Psychologist with the Health Professions Council. Experience of implementing and delivering offending behaviour programmes is essential, along with extensive experience of working as a psychologist in a forensic setting.
	To view full details about these vacancies, and for more information on the SPS, visit our website at www.sps.gov.uk
	Our latest Vacancies can be found in the Careers section.
Working Hours:	Full-time
Salary:	£26,321 to £40,054 pro rata, dependent on qualifications and experience, plus attractive benefits
Location:	Scotland

Author's comment: Whilst qualified candidates are preferred here I have included this advertisement because it gives an insight into the responsibilities that a non-qualified psychologist can have whilst in training. What do you know about Offending Behaviour Programmes (OBPs)? Would you consider researching which prison delivers which OBP? How would you find out this information? What does this advert mean by demonstrating experience of implementing and delivering OBPs?

Example NHS job advertisement accessed on internet 01.08.12

http://www.jobs.nhs.uk/showvac/GTi34A/1754986/912919188

I have included this advertisement to demonstrate that you will already need to have developed a set of skills and knowledge prior to gaining a post as an assistant psychologist. Although it can be confusing to understand this is the level that comes before a trainee psychologist position and the Assistant Psychologist or Psychological Assistant is the first step on the ladder into a psychology career after gaining other experience. Competition for assistant posts is fierce as well.

JOB DESCRIPTION

Job Title: Assistant Psychologist

Grade: Band 5

Hours/sessions: 37.5 hours

Based at: Ilford

Professionally Accountable
To: Consultant Psychologist (Adult Rehabilitation Unit).

Line Manager & Clinically   Clinical Lead Psychologist (Forensic Low Secure Unit)
Reporting to:

Working Relationships: Psychologists, Psychiatrists, Nurses, Occupational Therapists, Art therapists, Social Workers and community team leads.

Job Summary and Purpose

The post-holder will be based in the Inpatient Adult Rehabilitation and Forensic Low Secure Services, linked to Inpatient Psychology. This post will support and enhance the psychological rehabilitation of service-users working in two inpatient wards (Monet and Morris wards). Your key responsibilities will be in the role of Assistant Psychologist: to provide: psychological assessment and interventions under the clinical supervision of a registered psychologist, working independently according to a plan agreed with a registered psychologist and within the overall framework of the team and Trust policies and procedures. To assist in clinically related administration, conduct of audits, collection of statistics, development of audit and/or research projects, teaching and project work as required. Work in these services may include occasional exposure to unpleasant conditions, verbal abuse or hostility.

KEY AREAS OF RESPONSIBILITY:

Clinical

To assist in the psychological assessment of clients referred to psychology based on the appropriate use, interpretation of complex information from a variety of sources including a range of psychological / psychometric tests, self-report measures, and semi-structured interviews with service users and others involved in their care, under supervision of a Registered Psychologist.

To assist in the undertaking of Violence Risk Assessments, Sexual Violence Risk Assessments, and Stalking Assessments of service-users using evidence-based assessment tools under the supervision of an HCPC Registered Psychologist.

To assist qualified psychologists in the formulation and implementation of care plans involving the psychological treatment/management of clients problems, and to participate in the delivery of psychological interventions / agreed care plans arising from such formulation under the supervision of a Registered Psychologist.

To assist in the development and facilitation of psychological treatment groups as appropriate and under supervision as required.

To produce written reports of assessments carried out and communicate in a skilled and sensitive manner information concerning client care.

To provide psycho-educational approaches using recovery based models, stress-vulnerability or coping / relapse signs of psychosis, and / or harm minimisation in dual diagnosis and substance misuse as required.

To work with other members of the multi-disciplinary team in the review of client care and in preparation for care plan review meetings.

To undertake joint work with other clinical staff as required by the care plan based on psychological understanding of client problems.

To attend and contribute to multi-disciplinary team meetings, care plan reviews and case formulation meetings as appropriate.

To assist in the development and facilitation of psycho-educational / support groups for carers of forensic and rehabilitation service users.

Teaching, Training and Supervision

In accordance with good practice guidelines, the post holder receives regular clinical professional supervision, from a Registered Psychologist. This involves guidance and discussion of clinical work, research and service development. This should be in line with the British Psychological Society's, NELFT's and the psychology department's policies on supervision.

To utilise supervision regularly as agreed with supervisor.

To maintain own professional development and requirement to take part in appraisal and KSF process.

To undertake continued professional development in line with BPS recommendations in order to develop skills and competencies that assist in the delivery of current duties.

To assist qualified psychologists in the department in the delivery of training and provision of support to other professional groups in psychological care.

To attend mandatory security training required for working on the forensic ward.

To attend all mandatory training as required by Trust policy.

To participate, as appropriate, in the training of other Health Service personnel and staff from other agencies involved in the provision of services to service users.

Clinical Audit and Research and Service Development

To assist in the design and implementation of clinical audit / service related research.

Under the direction and guidance of a qualified psychologist to initiate and undertake research projects, including monitoring and evaluating services for service users and/or their families/carers.

Under the direction and guidance of a qualified psychologist, to undertake data collection and analysis, using appropriate statistical programmes.

Under the direction and guidance of a qualified psychologist provide reports and summaries of Clinical audits and research projects.

To undertake literature searches to assist qualified psychologists in their duties.

To assist in the design and implementation of service developments within psychology.

IT Responsibilities

To comply with Trust policy regarding the use of the intranet, intranet and e-mail and the requirements of the Freedom of Information Act.

To be familiar and competent in the use of mainstream IT packages.

To make appropriate use of test interpretation software packages in line with the test company's requirements.

Management

In liaison with relevant administrative staff, to ensure the proper maintenance of case records and the collection of appropriate statistical data.

In conjunction with other personnel, to be responsible for the security of the office and filing systems.

General

To maintain the highest standards of clinical record keeping including electronic data entry and recording, report writing and the responsible exercise of professional self-governance in accordance with professional codes of practice of the British Psychological Society and Trust policies and procedures.

To promote psychology and psychological services by the development and maintenance of constructive working relationships with service users, carers and Trust staff.

To maintain appropriate personal standards of conduct consistent with professional practice and Trust policy.

The post holder must at all times carry out his/her duties with regard to NELFT's Equality and Diversity at Work Policy/s.

To undertake specific administrative duties as required.

To assist in clinically related administration, audits, collection of statistics, development of audit and/or research projects teaching and project work.

To use an appropriate range of office IT packages

To ensure adherence to relevant health and safety standards and other policies within the Trust.

To perform other duties of a similar kind appropriate to the grade, which may be required from time to time by the Clinical Lead Psychologist and Consultant Psychologist.

WORKING ENVIRONMENT

Demand for the psychology service means that the working environment of the post-holder is frequently pressurised. The nature of the work involves difficult working conditions of an emotionally demanding nature, may be subject to verbal aggression and abuse, and occasionally threats of physical aggression. Occasionally, individual work with service users will take place without other staff immediately nearby. The post-holder will be aware of these issues and take all appropriate measures to reduce risks to themselves, service users and Trust staff, in accordance with Trust training.

PERSON SPECIFICATION

I have abbreviated the person specification here but the applicant is required to have a 2:1 degree in psychology and it is desirable that they have had training in violence risk assessment (such as HCR-20). It is essential that the applicant has an excellent knowledge of the Recovery Model. Do you know what this is? It is desirable that the applicant will have an understanding of psychosis and its impact on young people. Perhaps it would be beneficial here to seek out the NICE guidelines on psychosis?

Appendix 2

Useful Addresses:

The British Psychological Society
St Andrews House
48 Princess Road East
Leicester LE1 7DR
Tel: +44 (0)116 254 9568
Fax: +44 (0)116 227 1314
E-mail: enquiries@bps.org.uk
http://www.bps.org.uk/

Health & Care Professions Council
Park House
184 Kennington Park Road
London SE11 4BU
www.hpc-uk.org

Appendix 3

Useful web pages for those seeking job vacancies (This list is not intended to be exhaustive but gives you a range of potential websites to visit):

1) http://jobs.trovit.co.uk/jobs/assistant-psychologist

2) www.jobs.ac.uk/categories/psychology
This site advertises research jobs in the university sector

3) www.jobs.nhs.uk/
Self-explanatory site offering jobs in the NHS

4) www.psychminded.co.uk
Mental health and psychologist jobs

5) https://www21.i-grasp.com/fe/tpl_hmps03.asp?newms=se
Prison Psychology jobs

6) http://www.nacro.org.uk/header/work-for-us/
NACRO is a crime reduction charity. Volunteering opportunities to mentor young and adult prisoners before and after release from custody

7) http://www.partnershipsincare.co.uk/jobs.aspx
Independent sector hospitals with some forensic units

8) http://huntercombe.com/careers/current-opportunities/
Independent sector hospitals with some forensic units

9) www.yjb.gov.uk
Youth Justice Board

10) http://www.sacro.org.uk/
Scotland – Safeguarding Communities – Reducing Reoffending

11) http://careers.turning-point.co.uk/
Turning Point, a registered charity, is a national health and social care provider and offers support for substance misuse, learning disabilities and mental distress.

12) http://www.brookdalecare.co.uk/current-vacancies
Specialist autism care and support

13) http://www.alphahospitals.co.uk/services/
Alpha Hospitals is an independent health care provider that works in partnership with the NHS to provide specialist services for people with mental health problems.

14) http://www.stah.org/
St Andrews Healthcare

Appendix 4

Blog

http://forensicpsychtrainees.blogspot.co.uk/

Check out the useful articles on this blog aimed at forensic psychologists in training or those considering training

Appendix 5 – Additional resources and reading

http://www.nice.org.uk/

Search this website for clinical guidelines e.g. schizophrenia or borderline personality disorder

http://www.prisonreformtrust.org.uk/

According to their website the Prison Reform Trust (PRT) is an independent UK charity working to create a just, humane and effective penal system.

http://www.ohrn.nhs.uk/

Offender Health Research Network

http://www.clinpsy.org.uk/forum/

Information for people interested in careers in clinical psychology

References:

Adler, J.R., & Gray, J.M. (2010). *Forensic Psychology: Concepts, debates and practice*: Willan.

Alison, L. (Ed.). (2005). *The Forensic Psychologist's Casebook: Psychological profiling and criminal investigation*: Willan publishing.

Crighton, D.A. & Towl, G.J. (2008). *Psychology in Prisons* (2nd ed.): BPS Blackwell.

Forensic Update (2012). Annual Division of Forensic Psychology Survey, 2010-2011. British Psychological Society

Knight, A. (2002). *How to Become a Clinical Psychologist – Getting a foot in the door*. Hove: Brunner-Routledge.

Towl, G.J. (2006). *Psychological Research in Prisons*: BPS Blackwell.

2478033R00077

Printed in Germany
by Amazon Distribution
GmbH, Leipzig